taste of home
casseroles
slow cooker
& soups

BREAKFAST SUPREME, P. 10

MEAT LOAF BURGERS, P. 50

TORTILLA-VEGETABLE CHICKEN SOUP, P. 74

Cozy Family Meals Are Yours!

When you want good homemade food without sacrificing convenience, *Taste of Home Casseroles, Slow Cooker & Soups* is the cookbook you'll reach for time and again!

This collection gives you the easy-to-make, delicious family favorites you crave with thrifty, spirit-lifting casseroles, slow-cooked entrees, and one-pot soups and stews.

In the CASSEROLES chapter, you'll find warm, oven-baked goodness to take you through the day, from tempting breakfast bakes to dinnertime classics such as Double-Cheese Macaroni (p. 23) and Almond Chicken Casserole (p. 20).

Easy entertaining and effortless home-cooked meals are yours with the recipes in the SLOW COOKER chapter. Besides popular roasts, meat loaves, ribs and sandwiches, you'll find 18 recipes perfect for entertaining in the Appetizers & Beverages section. Party-favorite drinks, meatballs, dips and more...all with slow-cooker convenience and without taking up space on the stovetop or time away from your family and guests!

Nothing warms and comforts like SOUP on a chilly day, and you'll be cooking up satisfying vegetable soups, hearty stews, chowders, chili and more with this popular section. Some simmer for hours and others are done in just minutes, so these recipes are sure to fit your schedule. The hardest time you'll have is choosing which to try first!

Each recipe includes clear, step-by-step instructions and a full-color photo. Best of all, every dish was kitchen-tested and -approved so you know everything will turn out great! You hold the secret to great family meals in your hands with Casseroles, Slow Cooker & Soups. So what are you waiting for? Go ahead and dig in today!

taste of home
casseroles slow cooker & soups

EDITOR-IN-CHIEF:
Catherine Cassidy

VICE PRESIDENT, EXECUTIVE EDITOR/BOOKS:
Heidi Reuter Lloyd

CREATIVE DIRECTOR: Howard Greenberg

FOOD DIRECTOR: Diane Werner, RD

SENIOR EDITOR/BOOKS: Mark Hagen

ASSOCIATE EDITOR: Christine Rukavena

ASSOCIATE CREATIVE DIRECTOR:
Edwin Robles Jr.

ART DIRECTOR: Jessie Sharon

CONTENT PRODUCTION MANAGER:
Julie Wagner

LAYOUT DESIGNER: Nancy Novak

COPY CHIEF: Deb Warlaumont Mulvey

COPY EDITOR: Joanne Weintraub

RECIPE ASSET SYSTEM MANAGER:
Coleen Martin

RECIPE TESTING AND EDITING:
Taste of Home Test Kitchen

FOOD PHOTOGRAPHY:
Taste of Home Photo Studio

ADMINISTRATIVE ASSISTANT: Barb Czysz

COVER PHOTOGRAPHER: Rob Hagen

COVER FOOD STYLIST: Diane Armstrong

COVER SET STYLIST: Dolores Jacq

NORTH AMERICAN CHIEF MARKETING OFFICER: Lisa Karpinski

VICE PRESIDENT/BOOK MARKETING:
Dan Fink

CREATIVE DIRECTOR/CREATIVE MARKETING: Jim Palmen

**THE READER'S DIGEST ASSOCIATION, INC.
PRESIDENT AND CHIEF EXECUTIVE OFFICER:** Tom Williams

EXECUTIVE VICE PRESIDENT, RDA, AND PRESIDENT, LIFESTYLE COMMUNITIES:
Suzanne M. Grimes

©2011 Reiman Media Group, LLC
5400 S. 60th St., Greendale, WI 53129
All rights reserved.

Taste of Home is a registered trademark of
The Reader's Digest Association, Inc.

INTERNATIONAL STANDARD BOOK
NUMBER (10): 0-89821-890-X

INTERNATIONAL STANDARD BOOK
NUMBER (13): 978-0-89821-890-9

LIBRARY OF CONGRESS CONTROL
NUMBER: 2011921302

Printed in USA
3 5 7 9 10 8 6 4 2

PICTURED ON FRONT COVER:
Parmesan Penne (p. 25).

PICTURED ON BACK COVER:
Cheddar Turkey Bake (p. 27), Double-Onion
Beef Brisket (p. 70), Chicken Chowder (p. 93)
and Zippy Beef Fajitas (p. 58).

For other Taste of Home books and products,
visit ShopTasteofHome.com

table of contents

HEARTY MINESTRONE, P. 79

casseroles

« DOUBLE-CHEESE MACARONI, P. 23

egg biscuit bake

ALICE LE DUC
CEDARBURG, WISCONSIN

Convenient refrigerated biscuits create a golden border around this all-in-one meal. It's a variation of a simple egg-cheese combination my mother used to make.

1 can (5 ounces) evaporated milk
8 ounces process cheese (Velveeta), cubed
1 teaspoon prepared mustard
3/4 cup cubed fully cooked ham
1/2 cup frozen peas
2 tablespoons butter
10 eggs, lightly beaten
1 tube (12 ounces) refrigerated buttermilk biscuits

1 In a large saucepan, combine the milk, cheese and mustard; cook over low heat until smooth, stirring constantly. Stir in ham and peas.

2 Melt butter in a large skillet, heat butter until hot. Add eggs; cook and stir over medium heat until eggs are completely set. Add cheese sauce and stir gently.

3 Spoon into an ungreased shallow 2-qt. baking dish. Separate the biscuits and cut in half. Place with cut side down around outer edge of dish.

4 Bake, uncovered, at 375° for 15-20 minutes or until a knife inserted near the center comes out clean and biscuits are golden brown.

YIELD: 4-6 SERVINGS.

scrambled egg casserole

MARY ANNE MCWHIRTER
PEARLAND, TEXAS

This has become the brunch dish I'm known for. The recipe combines the favorite flavors of hearty old-time country breakfasts with the ease of a modern make-ahead dish.

CHEESE SAUCE:
2 tablespoons butter
7-1/2 teaspoons all-purpose flour
2 cups milk
1/2 teaspoon salt
1/8 teaspoon pepper
1 cup cubed process cheese (Velveeta)
1 cup cubed fully cooked ham
1/4 cup chopped green onions
3 tablespoons butter, melted
12 eggs, beaten
1 can (4 ounces) mushroom stems and pieces, drained

TOPPING:
1/4 cup melted butter
2-1/4 cups soft bread crumbs

1 To make cheese sauce, in a large skillet, melt butter; stir in flour and cook for 1 minute. Gradually stir in milk. Bring to a boil; cook and stir for 1-2 minutes or until thickened. Add the salt, pepper and cheese; stir until cheese melts. Set aside.

2 In a small skillet, saute ham and green onions in 3 tablespoons butter until onion is tender. Add eggs and cook over medium heat until eggs are set; stir in mushrooms and cheese sauce.

3 Spoon eggs into greased 13-in. x 9-in. baking pan. Combine topping ingredients; spread evenly over egg mixture. Cover; chill overnight. Uncover; bake at 350° for 30 minutes.

YIELD: 10-12 SERVINGS.

ham and egg breakfast casseroles

LISA POGUE
KEITHVILLE, LOUISIANA

I made this for my family one day as I tried using things up in my fridge. Even my picky children loved it!

1 pound large fresh mushrooms, coarsely chopped
1/3 cup butter, cubed
1/2 teaspoon Italian seasoning
1/8 teaspoon pepper
4 cups (16 ounces) shredded sharp cheddar cheese
1-3/4 cups cubed fully cooked ham
1/2 cup shredded Parmesan cheese
2 tablespoons all-purpose flour
24 eggs
2 cups heavy whipping cream
1 tablespoon Dijon mustard
1/8 teaspoon white pepper

1 In a Dutch oven, saute mushrooms in butter until tender. Add Italian seasoning and pepper; saute about 1 minute longer. Spread mushroom mixture evenly into two greased 13-in. x 9-in. baking dishes.

2 In a large bowl, combine the cheddar cheese, ham, Parmesan cheese and flour. Sprinkle over mushroom mixture. In another large bowl, whisk the eggs, cream, mustard and white pepper. Pour over cheese mixture.

3 Cover and freeze one casserole for up to 3 months. Bake remaining casserole, uncovered, at 350° for 30-35 minutes or until a knife inserted near the center comes out clean. Let stand for 10 minutes before cutting.

4 **To use frozen casserole:** Remove from the freezer 30 minutes before baking (do not thaw). Cover and bake at 350° for 55 minutes. Uncover; bake 15-20 minutes longer or until a knife inserted near the center comes out clean. Let stand for 10 minutes before cutting.

YIELD: 2 CASSEROLES (12 SERVINGS EACH).

simple summer squash bake

I often make a summer squash bake for brunch. I add some chopped peppers for variety and extra color, and to spark the flavor of the zucchini and crookneck squash. Try jalapeno, sweet red or green pepper, depending on your taste preferences.

MARGERY S., ASHLAND, OREGON

sunshine baked eggs

JANE ZIELINSKI
ROTTERDAM JUNCTION, NEW YORK

My son-in-law experimented with my standby recipe for eggs by adding cottage cheese and crushed pineapple. It's so delicious, we make these eggs all the time!

- 1 pound sliced bacon
- 14 eggs
- 1-1/3 cups 4% cottage cheese
- 1 can (8 ounces) crushed pineapple, drained
- 1 teaspoon vanilla extract

Minced fresh parsley, optional

1 In a large skillet, cook bacon over medium heat until crisp. With a slotted spoon, remove to paper towels; drain, reserving 2 tablespoons drippings. Crumble bacon.

2 In a large bowl, lightly beat eggs; add bacon and drippings, cottage cheese, pineapple and vanilla. Pour into greased 11-in. x 7-in. baking dish.

3 Bake, uncovered, at 350° for 40-45 minutes or until a knife inserted near the center comes out clean. Let stand for 5 minutes. If desired, sprinkle with parsley.

YIELD: 8 SERVINGS.

ham & cheese egg bake

LISA RENSHAW
KANSAS CITY, MISSOURI

This delectable dish could easily be served for breakfast, lunch or dinner. So simple to prepare, yet so comforting and scrumptious.

- 5 eggs
- 1/4 cup all-purpose flour
- 1/2 teaspoon baking powder
- 2 cups (8 ounces) shredded Havarti cheese
- 1 cup (4 ounces) shredded Swiss cheese
- 1 cup cubed fully cooked ham
- 1 cup ricotta cheese
- 1/4 cup butter, melted
- 2 tablespoons snipped fresh dill *or* 2 teaspoons dill weed
- 2 tablespoons Dijon mustard
- 1/2 teaspoon fennel seed

1 In a large bowl, beat eggs on medium-high speed for 2 minutes or until lemon-colored. Combine flour and baking powder; gradually add to eggs and mix well. Stir in the remaining ingredients.

2 Pour into a greased 11-in. x 7-in. baking dish. Bake, uncovered, at 375° for 24-28 minutes or until a knife inserted near the center comes out clean. Let stand for 5 minutes before cutting.

YIELD: 6 SERVINGS.

freeze cheese before shredding

Before shredding soft cheeses like mozzarella, I put the cheese in the freezer for about 30 minutes. I've found this makes it easier to shred, and the cheese doesn't stick to the grater.

CHERYL J., BELTSVILLE, MARYLAND

brunch enchiladas

PAT O'BRIEN
SOQUEL, CALIFORNIA

This dish takes me back to when my grandmother would visit. While she prepared one of her best meals, she'd give me dough to make my own tortillas. With such tasty memories, it's no surprise this is my favorite recipe!

- 2 cups ground fully cooked ham
- 1/2 cup sliced green onions
- 1/2 cup finely chopped green pepper
- 2 tablespoons canola oil
- 8 flour tortillas (8 inches)
- 2-1/2 cups (10 ounces) shredded cheddar cheese, *divided*
- 4 eggs
- 2 cups half-and-half cream
- 1 tablespoon all-purpose flour
- 1/4 teaspoon garlic powder
- 2 to 3 drops hot pepper sauce
- Salsa
- Sour cream

1 In a large skillet, saute the ham, onions and green pepper in oil until vegetables are tender. Place 1/3 cup down the center of each tortilla; top with 3 tablespoons cheese. Roll up and place seam side down in a greased 11-in. x 7-in. baking dish.

2 In a small bowl, whisk the eggs, cream, flour, garlic powder and hot pepper sauce. Pour over tortillas. Cover and chill 8 hours or overnight.

3 Remove from refrigerator 30 minutes before baking. Bake, uncovered, at 350° for 45-50 minutes or until a knife inserted near the center comes out clean. Let stand 5 minutes. Serve with salsa and sour cream.

YIELD: 4 SERVINGS.

maple french toast bake

CINDY STEFFEN
CEDARBURG, WISCONSIN

This yummy French toast casserole is a breeze to whip up the night before a busy morning. My family loves the richness it gets from cream cheese and maple syrup.

- 12 slices bread, cubed
- 1 package (8 ounces) cream cheese, cubed
- 8 eggs
- 1 cup milk
- 1/2 cup maple syrup
- Additional maple syrup

1 Arrange half of the bread cubes in a greased shallow 2-qt. baking dish. Top with cream cheese and remaining bread. In a large bowl, whisk the eggs, milk and syrup; pour over bread. Cover and refrigerate overnight. Remove from the refrigerator about 30 minutes before baking.

2 Cover and bake at 350° for 30 minutes. Uncover; bake 20-25 minutes longer or until golden brown. Serve with additional syrup.

YIELD: 8 SERVINGS.

ham vegetable strata

DIANE MEYER
GENESEO, NEW YORK

Ever since my niece gave me this recipe, I've shared it with many of my friends. The crunchy, golden-brown topping and colorful ingredients present a tantalizing dish. It's my favorite brunch entree to serve.

1 small zucchini, cut into 1/4-inch slices
2 cups fresh broccoli florets
1/2 cup shredded carrots
12 slices white bread, crusts removed
1 cup cubed fully cooked ham
1 can (8 ounces) mushroom stems and pieces, drained
1 cup (4 ounces) shredded sharp cheddar cheese
1 cup (4 ounces) shredded Swiss cheese
12 eggs
2-1/2 cups milk
1/4 cup chopped onion
1/2 teaspoon ground mustard
1/4 teaspoon salt
1/8 teaspoon pepper
1-1/2 cups crushed cornflakes
1/4 cup butter, melted

1 In a small saucepan, cook the zucchini, broccoli and carrots in 1 in. of water for 5-10 minutes or until tender; drain. Meanwhile, cut bread in half diagonally; place half of the pieces in a greased 13-in. x 9-in. baking dish. Top with half of the vegetables, ham, mushrooms and cheeses. Repeat layers. In a large bowl, whisk the eggs, milk, onion, mustard, salt and pepper; pour over the ham mixture. Cover and refrigerate for 8 hours or overnight.

2 Remove from the refrigerator 30 minutes before baking. Toss cornflakes and butter; sprinkle over the casserole. Bake, uncovered, at 350° for 50-60 minutes or until a knife inserted near the center comes out clean. Let stand for 10 minutes before cutting.

YIELD: 12-16 SERVINGS.

breakfast supreme

LAURIE HARMS
GRINNELL, IOWA

Friends shared this recipe with me many years ago when we spent the night at their home. After one taste, you'll understand why this breakfast is "supreme." It's really that good!

1 pound bulk pork sausage
1 pound ground beef
1 small onion, chopped
3/4 cup sliced fresh mushrooms
1/2 cup chopped green pepper
1 to 1-1/2 teaspoons salt
1/4 to 1/2 teaspoon pepper
2 tablespoons butter, melted
2 cups (8 ounces) shredded cheddar cheese, *divided*
12 eggs
2/3 cup heavy whipping cream

1 In a large skillet, cook the sausage, beef, onion, mushrooms and green pepper over medium heat until meat is no longer pink; drain. Stir in salt and pepper; set aside.

2 Pour butter into an ungreased 13-in. x 9-in. baking dish. Sprinkle with 1 cup cheese. Beat eggs; pour over cheese. Top with sausage mixture.

3 Pour the cream over sausage mixture. Sprinkle with remaining cheese. Cover and refrigerate for 8 hours or overnight.

4 Remove from the refrigerator 30 minutes before baking. Bake, uncovered, at 325° for 35-40 minutes or until a knife inserted near the center comes out clean. Let stand for 10 minutes before cutting.

YIELD: 12 SERVINGS.

lattice sausage pie

JENNIFER POLK
LINCOLN, NEBRASKA

I often serve this hearty egg dish to family and guests for special occasions. They rave over the flavor. A tube of refrigerated crescent rolls makes a tasty and easy crust.

- 2 tubes (8 ounces *each*) refrigerated crescent rolls
- 12 ounces pork sausage links, cooked and cut into 1/2-inch pieces
- 1 medium onion, chopped
- 1 tablespoon butter
- 1 jar (4-1/2 ounces) sliced mushrooms, drained
- 2 packages (3 ounces *each*) cream cheese, cut into 1/4-inch cubes
- 4 ounces process cheese (Velveeta), cut into 1/4-inch cubes
- 2 tablespoons chopped pimientos
- 6 eggs
- 2/3 cup half-and-half cream
- 1 tablespoon dried parsley flakes
- 1/2 teaspoon salt
- 1/2 teaspoon pepper
- 1/2 teaspoon garlic powder

Paprika

1 Unroll one tube of crescent roll dough; press onto the bottom and up the sides of a greased 11-in. x 7-in. baking dish to form a crust. Seal seams and perforations. Sprinkle sausage over crust.

2 In a small skillet, saute onion in butter until tender; add the mushrooms. Spoon over sausage. Top with cheeses and pimientos. In a large bowl, whisk the eggs, cream, parsley, salt, pepper and garlic powder; pour over all.

3 Unroll the remaining dough; seal seams and perforations. Cut into 1/2-in. lengthwise strips. Use strips to form a lattice crust on top. Sprinkle with paprika.

4 Bake at 350° for 50-55 minutes or until knife inserted near the center comes out clean. Cover loosely with foil if top browns too quickly. Let stand for 10-15 minutes before cutting.

YIELD: 8-10 SERVINGS.

asparagus strata

AMY GROVER
SALEM, MASSACHUSETTS

The original recipe for this wonderful egg dish called for sausage, but fresh asparagus is tasty—and healthier for you, too!

- 4 cups water
- 1 pound fresh asparagus, trimmed and cut into 1/2-inch pieces
- 2 cups 2% milk
- 6 bread slices, crusts removed, cubed
- 6 eggs, lightly beaten
- 1 cup (4 ounces) shredded cheddar cheese
- 1 teaspoon salt

1 In a large saucepan, bring water to a boil. Add asparagus; boil, uncovered, for 3 minutes. Drain and immediately place asparagus in ice water. Drain and pat dry.

2 In a large bowl, combine the asparagus, milk, bread cubes, eggs, cheese and salt. Transfer to a greased 2-qt. baking dish. Cover and refrigerate for 5 hours or overnight.

3 Remove from the refrigerator 30 minutes before baking. Bake, uncovered, at 350° for 45-55 minutes or until a knife inserted near the center comes out clean.

YIELD: 6 SERVINGS.

spring-ahead brunch bake

LOIS JACOBSEN
DALLAS, WISCONSIN

The great taste of this enchilada-style dish makes it popular with my family. The fact that it can be made ahead makes it a hit with me.

- 2 cups sliced fresh mushrooms
- 1/2 cup sliced green onions
- 1/2 cup chopped green pepper
- 2 tablespoons butter
- 8 slices deli ham
- 8 flour tortillas (7 inches), warmed
- 1-1/2 cups (6 ounces) shredded Swiss cheese
- 1/2 cup shredded cheddar cheese
- 1 tablespoon all-purpose flour
- 4 eggs
- 2 cups milk
- 1/4 teaspoon garlic powder
- 1/4 teaspoon salt
- 1/8 teaspoon hot pepper sauce

1 In a large skillet, saute the mushrooms, onions and green pepper in butter until tender; set aside. Place one slice of ham on each tortilla. Top each with about 1/4 cup mushroom mixture. Combine cheeses; set aside 1/4 cup. Sprinkle remaining cheese over tortillas.

2 Roll up tortillas. Place seam side down in a greased 11-in. x 7-in. baking dish. In a large bowl, beat the flour, eggs, milk, garlic powder, salt and hot pepper sauce until blended.

3 Pour over tortillas. Sprinkle with reserved cheese. Cover and refrigerate for at least 30 minutes.

4 Bake, uncovered, at 350° for 35-45 minutes or until set.

YIELD: 8 SERVINGS.

easy ham hash

ESTHER JOHNSON DANIELSON
GREENVILLE, TEXAS

As the oldest of six children, I learned to cook early in life. Now my files are bulging with a variety of recipes. This delicious casserole remains a standby at my house.

- 1 pound finely ground fully cooked ham
- 1 large onion, finely chopped
- 3 medium potatoes, peeled and cooked
- 2 tablespoons butter, melted
- 2 tablespoons grated Parmesan cheese
- 1 tablespoon prepared mustard
- 2 teaspoons Worcestershire sauce
- 1 teaspoon prepared horseradish
- 1/4 teaspoon pepper
- 1 cup (4 ounces) shredded cheddar cheese
- 1/2 cup shredded Monterey Jack cheese

1 In a large bowl, combine ham and onion. Shred potatoes and add to ham mixture. Add the butter, Parmesan cheese, mustard, Worcestershire sauce, horseradish and pepper; mix well.

2 Spoon into a greased 11-in. x 7-in. baking dish, pressing down firmly. Combine remaining cheeses; sprinkle over the top. Bake, uncovered, at 350° for 35-40 minutes or until bubbly and cheese is melted.

YIELD: 6 SERVINGS.

tomato and cheese strata

MOLLY SEIDEL
EDGEWOOD, NEW MEXICO

This is a great make-ahead dish for brunch or supper. It's delicious! People who try it always ask me for the recipe.

- 10 slices white bread
- 4 medium tomatoes, sliced 1/2 inch thick
- 1 cup (4 ounces) shredded cheddar cheese
- 4 green onions, thinly sliced
- 4 eggs
- 2 cups milk
- 1/2 teaspoon salt

1 Line a greased 8-in. square baking dish with four bread slices. Layer with half of the tomatoes, cheese and onions. Top with remaining bread (slices will overlap). Layer with remaining tomatoes, cheese and onions.

2 In a small bowl, whisk the eggs, milk and salt. Pour over the top. Cover and refrigerate overnight.

3 Remove from the refrigerator 30 minutes before baking. Bake, uncovered, at 350° for 45-50 minutes or until a knife inserted near the center comes out clean. Let stand for 5 minutes before cutting.

YIELD: 4-6 SERVINGS.

preparing a successful and relaxed brunch

When choosing brunch recipes, look for some make-ahead choices as well as some last-minute dishes. The day before your brunch, iron tablecloths and napkins, set the table and put out serving dishes and utensils. Get a head start on as many dishes as possible by chopping, slicing and dicing the night before. Measure the coffee the night before. Then make it in the morning and transfer it to a thermal carafe for serving. Make and refrigerate the juice. In the morning, transfer it to a pretty pitcher. Review your menu and make a list of what needs to be done in the morning before guests arrive.

TASTE OF HOME TEST KITCHEN

cajun-style brunch bake

KATHIE DEUSSER
CHURCH POINT, LOUISIANA

It's so handy to fix this filling breakfast casserole the night before and refrigerate it until morning. It was given to me by a coworker and has turned out to be a family hit!

- 6 eggs, lightly beaten
- 2 cups 2% milk
- 1 pound sliced bacon, cooked and crumbled
- 6 slices bread, cubed
- 1 medium potato, peeled and diced
- 1 cup (4 ounces) shredded cheddar cheese
- 1/2 cup finely chopped onion
- 1 to 1-1/2 teaspoons Cajun seasoning
- 1 teaspoon salt

1 In a large bowl, combine all ingredients. Transfer to a greased 11-in. x 7-in. baking dish. Cover and refrigerate overnight.

2 Remove from the refrigerator 30 minutes before baking. Bake, uncovered, at 350° for 45-50 minutes or until a knife inserted near the center comes out clean. Let stand for 10 minutes before cutting.

YIELD: 6 SERVINGS.

taco quiche

KIM STOLLER
SMITHVILLE, OHIO

I always take this dish to potlucks, and the pan comes home empty every time. It's a stick-to-your-ribs casserole that has the taco flavor everyone just loves.

- 2 pounds ground beef
- 2 envelopes taco seasoning
- 4 eggs
- 3/4 cup milk
- 1-1/4 cups biscuit/baking mix
- Dash pepper
- 1/2 cup sour cream
- 2 to 3 cups chopped lettuce
- 3/4 cup chopped tomato
- 1/4 cup chopped green pepper
- 1/4 cup chopped green onions
- 2 cups (8 ounces) shredded cheddar cheese

1 In a large skillet, cook beef over medium heat until no longer pink; drain. Add taco seasoning and prepare according to the package directions. Spoon meat into a greased 13-in. x 9-in. baking dish.

2 In a large bowl, beat eggs and milk. Stir in biscuit mix and pepper. Pour over meat. Bake, uncovered, at 400° for 20-25 minutes or until golden brown. Cool for 5-10 minutes. Spread sour cream over the top; sprinkle with lettuce, tomato, green pepper, onions and cheese. Serve immediately.

YIELD: 8 SERVINGS.

double-cheese ziti with bacon

TASTE OF HOME TEST KITCHEN

This mac and cheese is real comfort food. No one can resist the combination of cheesy pasta, golden bread crumbs and bacon!

- 1 package (16 ounces) ziti *or* small tube pasta
- 3 cups (24 ounces) 4% cottage cheese
- 1/2 cup plus 1 tablespoon butter, *divided*
- 1/2 cup all-purpose flour
- 1 teaspoon salt
- 1/2 teaspoon white pepper
- 1/4 teaspoon garlic salt
- 3 cups half-and-half cream
- 1 cup milk
- 4 cups (16 ounces) shredded cheddar cheese
- 1 cup crumbled cooked bacon, *divided*
- 1/3 cup dry bread crumbs

1 Cook pasta according to package directions. Meanwhile, place cottage cheese in a food processor; cover and process until smooth. Set aside.

2 In a large saucepan, melt 1/2 cup butter. Stir in the flour, salt, pepper and garlic salt until smooth. Gradually add cream and milk. Bring to a boil; cook and stir for 2 minutes or until thickened.

3 Drain pasta; transfer to a large bowl. Add the cheddar cheese, cottage cheese, white sauce and 3/4 cup bacon; toss to coat. Transfer to a greased 13-in. x 9-in. baking dish. (Dish will be full.) Melt remaining butter. Add bread crumbs; toss to coat. Sprinkle over casserole.

4 Bake, uncovered, at 400° for 20 minutes. Sprinkle with the remaining bacon. Bake 5 minutes longer or until bubbly.

YIELD: 12 SERVINGS (1 CUP EACH).

hot chicken salad

BERNICE KNUTSON
DANBURY, IOWA

The whole family will love this creamy mix of crunchy veggies and hot chicken topped with crispy potato chips. You'll adore the quick and easy prep!

- 1 package (9 ounces) frozen diced cooked chicken breast, thawed
- 2 cups thinly sliced celery
- 1 can (8 ounces) sliced water chestnuts, drained
- 1/2 cup chopped almonds
- 1/3 cup chopped green pepper
- 1 jar (2 ounces) diced pimientos, drained
- 2 tablespoons finely chopped onion
- 2/3 cup shredded Swiss cheese, *divided*
- 1 cup mayonnaise
- 2 tablespoons lemon juice
- 1/2 teaspoon salt
- 2 cups crushed potato chips

1 In a large bowl, combine the chicken, celery, water chestnuts, almonds, green pepper, pimientos, onion and 1/3 cup cheese. In a small bowl, combine the mayonnaise, lemon juice and salt. Stir into chicken mixture and toss to coat.

2 Transfer to a greased 8-in. square baking dish. Bake, uncovered, at 350° for 20 minutes.

3 Sprinkle with potato chips and remaining cheese. Bake 10-15 minutes longer or until heated through and cheese is melted.

YIELD: 4 SERVINGS.

beef and potato moussaka

JEAN PUFFER
CHILLIWACK, BRITISH COLUMBIA

My son brought home this recipe for moussaka (a classic Greek entree) when he had a sixth-grade assignment about Greece. It earned high marks when we made it for his class.

- 1 pound ground beef
- 1 medium onion, chopped
- 1 garlic clove, minced
- 3/4 cup water
- 1 can (6 ounces) tomato paste
- 3 tablespoons minced fresh parsley
- 1 teaspoon salt
- 1/2 teaspoon dried mint, optional
- 1/4 teaspoon ground cinnamon
- 1/4 teaspoon pepper

PARMESAN SAUCE:

- 1/4 cup butter, cubed
- 1/4 cup all-purpose flour
- 2 cups milk
- 4 eggs, lightly beaten
- 1/2 cup grated Parmesan cheese
- 1/2 teaspoon salt
- 5 medium potatoes, peeled and thinly sliced

1 In a large skillet, cook beef and onion over medium heat until meat is no longer pink. Add garlic; cook 1 minute longer. Drain. Stir in the water, tomato paste, parsley, salt, mint if desired, cinnamon and pepper. Set aside.

2 For sauce, melt butter in a saucepan over medium heat. Stir in flour until smooth; gradually add milk. Bring to a boil; cook and stir for 2 minutes or until thickened. Remove from the heat. Stir a small amount of hot mixture into eggs; return all to the pan, stirring constantly. Add cheese and salt.

3 Place half of the potato slices in a greased shallow 3-qt. baking dish. Top with half of the cheese sauce and all of the meat mixture. Arrange the remaining potatoes over meat mixture; top with the remaining cheese sauce.

4 Bake, uncovered, at 350° for 1 hour or until a meat thermometer reads 160°. Let stand for 10 minutes before serving.

YIELD: 8-10 SERVINGS.

nacho cheese beef bake

KENDRA MCINTYRE
WEBSTER, SOUTH DAKOTA

My daughter came up with this recipe when she was visiting her fiance's family. Her future father-in-law thought she was a pretty good cook after sampling it!

- 2 cups uncooked egg noodles
- 1 pound ground beef
- 1 can (14-1/2 ounces) diced tomatoes
- 1 can (10-3/4 ounces) condensed nacho cheese soup, undiluted
- 1 jar (5-3/4 ounces) sliced pimiento-stuffed olives, drained
- 1 can (4 ounces) chopped green chilies
- 1-1/2 cups (6 ounces) shredded cheddar cheese
- 2 cups crushed tortilla chips
- 1/3 cup prepared ranch salad dressing
- Shredded lettuce, sour cream *and/or* salsa, optional

1 Cook noodles according to package directions; drain. Meanwhile, in a large saucepan, cook beef over medium heat until no longer pink; drain. Stir in the tomatoes, soup, olives and chilies. Bring to a boil. Reduce heat; simmer, uncovered, for 10 minutes. Stir in noodles.

2 Transfer to a greased 11-in. x 7-in. baking dish. Sprinkle with cheese. Bake at 350° for 15-20 minutes or until heated through. Top with tortilla chips; drizzle with salad dressing. Serve with lettuce, sour cream and/or salsa if desired.

YIELD: 4 SERVINGS.

chicken spaghetti casserole

BERNICE JANOWSKI
STEVENS POINT, WISCONSIN

I first made this meal-in-one when I had unexpected guests. It's popular when I'm in a hurry, because it takes only minutes to assemble.

- 8 ounces uncooked spaghetti
- 1 cup ricotta cheese
- 1 cup (4 ounces) shredded part-skim mozzarella cheese, *divided*
- 2 tablespoons grated Parmesan cheese
- 1/2 teaspoon Italian seasoning
- 1/2 teaspoon garlic powder
- 1 jar (26 ounces) meatless spaghetti sauce
- 1 can (14-1/2 ounces) Italian diced tomatoes, undrained
- 1 jar (4-1/2 ounces) sliced mushrooms, drained
- 4 fully cooked breaded chicken patties (10 to 14 ounces)

1 Cook spaghetti according to package directions. Meanwhile, in a large bowl, combine the ricotta, 1/2 cup of mozzarella, Parmesan, Italian seasoning and garlic powder; set aside. In another bowl, combine the spaghetti sauce, tomatoes and mushrooms.

2 Drain spaghetti; add 2 cups spaghetti sauce mixture and toss to coat. Transfer to a greased 13-in. x 9-in. baking dish; top with cheese mixture.

3 Arrange chicken patties over the top; drizzle with the remaining spaghetti sauce mixture. Sprinkle with the remaining mozzarella. Bake, uncovered, at 350° for 40-45 minutes or until bubbly.

YIELD: 4 SERVINGS.

southwest tuna noodle bake

SANDRA CRANE
LAS CRUCES, NEW MEXICO

None of my co-workers had ever tried tuna noodle casserole. Since we live near the Mexican border, they challenged me to make my version Southwestern. After trying this dish, everyone wanted the recipe!

- 1 package (16 ounces) egg noodles
- 2-1/2 cups milk
- 2 cans (6 ounces *each*) light water-packed tuna, drained
- 1 can (10-3/4 ounces) condensed cream of chicken soup, undiluted
- 1 can (10-3/4 ounces) condensed cream of mushroom soup, undiluted
- 1 cup (4 ounces) shredded cheddar cheese
- 1 can (4 ounces) chopped green chilies
- 2 cups crushed tortilla chips

1 Cook noodles according to package directions. Meanwhile, in a large bowl, combine the milk, tuna, soups, cheese and chilies. Drain noodles; gently stir into tuna mixture.

2 Transfer to an ungreased 13-in. x 9-in. baking dish. Sprinkle with tortilla chips. Bake, uncovered, at 350° for 30-35 minutes or until bubbly.

YIELD: 6 SERVINGS.

pizza casserole

NANCY ZIMMERMAN
CAPE MAY COURT HOUSE, NEW JERSEY

Looking for a satisfying dish the whole gang will love? This fast and flavorful pizza entree fills my home with a wonderful aroma. Refrigerated breadsticks make the crust fuss-free, and any leftovers freeze well for another busy day.

- 3/4 cup chopped onion
- 1 medium sweet yellow pepper, diced
- 1 medium sweet red pepper, diced
- 1 tablespoon olive oil
- 1 medium zucchini, halved lengthwise and sliced
- 1 teaspoon minced garlic
- 2 cans (14-1/2 ounces *each*) diced tomatoes, drained
- 3/4 pound smoked sausage, sliced
- 1 can (6 ounces) tomato paste
- 1 teaspoon salt
- 1 teaspoon Italian seasoning
- 1/2 teaspoon pepper
- 1/4 cup grated Parmesan cheese, *divided*
- 2 cups (8 ounces) shredded part-skim mozzarella cheese
- 1 tube (11 ounces) refrigerated breadsticks

1 In a large skillet, saute onion and peppers in oil for 2-3 minutes or until crisp-tender. Add zucchini and garlic; saute 4-6 minutes longer or until vegetables are tender. Stir in the tomatoes, sausage, tomato paste, salt, Italian seasoning, pepper and 2 tablespoons Parmesan cheese. Bring to a boil. Reduce heat; simmer, uncovered, for 8-10 minutes or until heated through.

2 Spoon half of the sausage mixture into a greased 13-in. x 9-in. baking dish. Sprinkle with mozzarella cheese; top with remaining sausage mixture. Separate breadsticks; arrange in a lattice pattern over the top. Sprinkle with remaining Parmesan cheese.

3 Bake, uncovered, at 375° for 25-30 minutes or until topping is golden brown and filling is bubbly. Let stand for 10 minutes before serving.

YIELD: 6-8 SERVINGS.

almond chicken casserole

MICHELLE KRZMARCZICK
REDONDO BEACH, CALIFORNIA

This mouthwatering casserole makes an excellent potluck dish. It's creamy and bursting with flavor. A golden topping made of cornflakes and almonds offers the perfect amount of crunch!

- 2 cups cubed cooked chicken
- 1 can (10-3/4 ounces) condensed cream of chicken soup, undiluted
- 1 cup (8 ounces) sour cream
- 3/4 cup mayonnaise
- 2 celery ribs, chopped
- 3 hard-cooked eggs, chopped
- 1 can (4 ounces) mushroom stems and pieces, drained
- 1 can (8 ounces) water chestnuts, drained and chopped
- 1 tablespoon finely chopped onion
- 2 teaspoons lemon juice
- 1/2 teaspoon salt
- 1/4 teaspoon pepper
- 1 cup (4 ounces) shredded cheddar cheese
- 1/2 cup crushed cornflakes
- 2 tablespoons butter, melted
- 1/4 cup sliced almonds

1 In a large bowl, combine the first 12 ingredients. Transfer to a greased 13-in. x 9-in. baking dish; sprinkle with cheese.

2 Toss cornflakes with butter; sprinkle over cheese. Top with almonds. Bake, uncovered, at 350° for 25-30 minutes or until heated through.

YIELD: 6-8 SERVINGS.

hearty pizza casserole

BARBARA WALKER
BROOKVILLE, KANSAS

My cheesy, meaty meal-in-one is easy to make and can be prepared ahead of time. Add salad and bread for an amazing meal.

- 1 cup uncooked elbow macaroni
- 1/2 pound lean ground beef (90% lean)
- 6 small fresh mushrooms, halved
- 1/3 cup chopped onion
- 1 can (8 ounces) tomato sauce
- 1 package (3-1/2 ounces) sliced pepperoni
- 2 tablespoons sliced ripe olives
- 1 teaspoon sugar
- 3/4 teaspoon Italian seasoning
- 1/4 teaspoon pepper
- 1/4 cup shredded cheddar cheese
- 1/4 cup shredded part-skim mozzarella cheese

1 Cook macaroni according to package directions. Meanwhile, in a large skillet, cook the beef, mushrooms and onion over medium heat until meat is no longer pink; drain. Stir in the tomato sauce, pepperoni, olives, sugar, Italian seasoning and pepper.

2 Drain macaroni; add to meat mixture. Transfer to a 1-1/2-qt. baking dish coated with cooking spray. Sprinkle with cheeses.

3 Bake uncovered at 350° for 20-25 minutes or until heated through.

YIELD: 4 SERVINGS.

artichoke shrimp bake

JEANNE HOLT
SAINT PAUL, MINNESOTA

I usually serve this dish with rice or baking powder biscuits. You can substitute frozen asparagus cuts for the artichokes and cream of asparagus soup for cream of shrimp.

- 1 pound cooked medium shrimp, peeled and deveined
- 1 can (14 ounces) water-packed quartered artichoke hearts, rinsed, drained and quartered
- 2/3 cup frozen pearl onions, thawed
- 2 cups sliced fresh mushrooms
- 1 small sweet red pepper, chopped
- 2 tablespoons butter
- 1 can (10-3/4 ounces) condensed cream of shrimp soup, undiluted
- 1/2 cup sour cream
- 1/4 cup sherry *or* chicken broth
- 2 teaspoons Worcestershire sauce
- 1 teaspoon grated lemon peel
- 1/8 teaspoon white pepper

TOPPING:
- 1/2 cup soft bread crumbs
- 1/3 cup grated Parmesan cheese
- 1 tablespoon minced fresh parsley
- 1 tablespoon butter, melted

Hot cooked rice, optional

1 Place the shrimp, artichokes and onions in a greased 11-in. x 7-in. baking dish; set aside. In a large skillet, saute mushrooms and red pepper in butter until tender. Stir in the soup, sour cream, sherry or broth, Worcestershire sauce, lemon peel and white pepper; heat through. Pour over shrimp mixture.

2 In a small bowl, combine the bread crumbs, Parmesan, parsley and butter; sprinkle over top.

3 Bake, uncovered, at 375° for 20-25 minutes or until bubbly and topping is golden brown. Serve with rice if desired.

YIELD: 4 SERVINGS.

brat 'n' tot bake

JODI GOBRECHT
BUCYRUS, OHIO

As a volunteer at our annual Bratwurst Festival, I could not have someone in my family who disliked bratwurst, so I developed this cheesy casserole.

- 1 pound uncooked bratwurst links, casings removed
- 1 medium onion, chopped
- 1 can (10-3/4 ounces) condensed cream of mushroom soup, undiluted
- 1 package (32 ounces) frozen Tater Tots
- 2 cups (16 ounces) sour cream
- 2 cups (8 ounces) shredded cheddar cheese

1 Crumble bratwurst into a large skillet; add onion. Cook over medium heat until meat is no longer pink; drain. Stir in the soup.

2 Transfer to a greased 13-in. x 9-in. baking dish. Top with Tater Tots and sour cream. Sprinkle with cheese. Bake, uncovered, at 350° for 35-40 minutes or until heated through and cheese is melted. Let stand for 5 minutes before serving.

YIELD: 6 SERVINGS.

ham 'n' cheese pasta

KAREN KOPP
INDIANAPOLIS, INDIANA

My mother would prepare this yummy comfort food whenever there was leftover ham. Horseradish gives it a nice tangy taste. I quickened the preparation by using process cheese instead of making a cheese sauce from scratch. Now my kids love it, too. This recipe can easily be doubled.

- 8 ounces uncooked medium pasta shells
- 1 pound process cheese (Velveeta), cubed
- 1/2 cup milk
- 2 tablespoons ketchup
- 1 tablespoon prepared horseradish
- 2 cups cubed fully cooked ham
- 1 package (8 ounces) frozen peas, thawed

1 Cook pasta according to package directions. Meanwhile, in a microwave-safe bowl, combine cheese and milk. Cover and microwave on high for 2 minutes; stir. Heat 1-2 minutes longer or until smooth, stirring twice. Stir in ketchup and horseradish until blended.

2 Drain pasta and place in a large bowl. Stir in the ham, peas and cheese sauce. Transfer to a greased 2-qt. baking dish. Cover and bake at 350° for 30-35 minutes or until bubbly.

YIELD: 4 SERVINGS.

add a little horseradish

When I serve applesauce with pork for a meal with guests, I add a touch of prepared horseradish. It's delicious.

CAROL D., SEMINOLE, FLORIDA

double-cheese macaroni

SABRINA DEWITT
CUMBERLAND, MARYLAND

A friend passed this recipe on to me, and I made some changes that resulted in a real crowd-pleaser. I make it for every get-together, and I haven't found anyone, child or adult, who doesn't love the ooey-gooey macaroni and cheese.

> 1 package (16 ounces) elbow macaroni
> 3 cups (24 ounces) 4% cottage cheese
> 1/2 cup butter, cubed
> 1/2 cup all-purpose flour
> 1 teaspoon salt
> 1/2 teaspoon white pepper
> 1/4 teaspoon garlic salt
> 3 cups half-and-half cream
> 1 cup milk
> 4 cups (16 ounces) shredded cheddar cheese

TOPPING:

> 1 cup dry bread crumbs
> 1/4 cup butter, melted

1 Cook macaroni according to package directions. Meanwhile, place cottage cheese in a food processor; cover and process until smooth. Set aside.

2 In a large saucepan, melt butter. Stir in the flour, salt, pepper and garlic salt until smooth. Gradually add cream and milk. Bring to a boil; cook and stir for 2 minutes or until thickened.

3 Drain macaroni; transfer to a large bowl. Add the cheddar cheese, cottage cheese and white sauce; toss to coat. Transfer to a greased 13-in. x 9-in. baking dish. (Dish will be full.) Combine bread crumbs and butter; sprinkle over the top.

4 Bake, uncovered, at 400° for 20-25 minutes or until bubbly.

YIELD: 12 SERVINGS (1 CUP EACH).

pepped up mac 'n' cheese

I add peeled tomatoes that have been drained and cut up, chopped onion and garlic powder to my macaroni and cheese—as my grandmother does. Just bake to warm through. It's delicious.

DEBBIE M., PASADENA, MARYLAND

meatball & sausage dinner

ELIZABETH MARTZ
PLEASANT GAP, PENNSYLVANIA

One day I was having trouble deciding what to make for dinner. So I combined whatever was in the refrigerator and freezer! To my surprise, everyone loved the result!

- 3 cups frozen chopped broccoli, thawed
- 2 medium potatoes, peeled and cubed
- 3 medium carrots, sliced
- 1 medium onion, chopped
- 1 pound smoked kielbasa *or* Polish sausage, halved and cut into 1-inch pieces
- 1/2 pound lean ground beef
- 1 can (14-1/2 ounces) beef broth
- Lemon-pepper seasoning to taste

1 In a large bowl, combine the first four ingredients. Transfer to a greased 13-in. x 9-in. baking pan. Sprinkle with sausage.

1 Shape beef into 1-in. balls; arrange over top. Pour broth over the casserole. Sprinkle with lemon-pepper. Bake, uncovered, at 350° for 1 hour or until meatballs are no longer pink.

YIELD: 6-8 SERVINGS.

creamy lasagna casserole

SHELLY KORELL
EATON, COLORADO

Satisfy your gang with this yummy casserole. A rich combination of cream cheese, sour cream and cheddar cheese is layered with lasagna noodles and a hearty, meaty sauce.

- 2 pounds ground beef
- 1 can (29 ounces) tomato sauce
- 1 teaspoon salt
- 1/2 teaspoon pepper
- 1/2 teaspoon garlic powder
- 2 packages (3 ounces *each*) cream cheese, softened
- 2 cups (16 ounces) sour cream
- 2 cups (8 ounces) shredded cheddar cheese, *divided*
- 4 green onions, chopped
- 12 to 14 lasagna noodles, cooked and drained

1 In a Dutch oven, cook beef over medium heat until no longer pink; drain. Add the tomato sauce, salt, pepper and garlic powder. Bring to a boil. Reduce heat; simmer, uncovered, for 15 minutes.

2 In a large bowl, beat cream cheese until smooth. Add the sour cream, 1 cup cheddar cheese and onions; mix well.

3 Spread about 1/2 cup meat sauce into two greased 8-in. square baking dishes. Place two to three noodles in each dish, trimming to fit if necessary. Top each with about 1/2 cup cream cheese mixture and about 2/3 cup meat sauce. Repeat layers twice. Sprinkle 1/2 cup cheddar cheese over each.

4 Cover and freeze one casserole for up to 1 month. Bake remaining casserole, uncovered, at 350° for 25-30 minutes or until bubbly and heated through. Let stand for 15 minutes before cutting.

5 **To use frozen casserole:** Thaw in the refrigerator for 18 hours. Remove casserole from the refrigerator 30 minutes before baking. Bake, uncovered, at 350° for 40-50 minutes or until heated through.

YIELD: 2 CASSEROLES (4-6 SERVINGS EACH).

EDITOR'S NOTES: Reduced-fat or fat-free cream cheese and sour cream are not recommended for this recipe.

parmesan penne

VERA SOGHOMONIAN
MAPLE GROVE, MINNESOTA

Here's a meal-in-one pasta with both a creamy Parmesan sauce and a tomato meat sauce. My husband has always encouraged me to experiment in the kitchen. This is one tasty result.

- 1 pound ground beef
- 1 medium onion, chopped
- 1 can (28 ounces) tomato sauce
- 1 cup grated Parmesan cheese, *divided*
- 1/2 teaspoon ground allspice

Salt and pepper to taste

- 1 package (16 ounces) penne pasta
- 1/2 cup butter, cubed, *divided*
- 1/4 cup all-purpose flour
- 2 cups milk
- 2 eggs, lightly beaten

1 In a large skillet, cook and stir beef and onion over medium heat until meat is no longer pink; drain. Stir in the tomato sauce, 1/3 cup cheese, allspice, salt and pepper. Bring to a boil. Reduce heat; simmer, uncovered, for 15 minutes.

2 Meanwhile, cook pasta according to package directions. In a large saucepan, melt 1/4 cup butter. Stir in flour until smooth. Gradually add milk. Bring to a boil; cook and stir for 2 minutes or until thickened. Remove from the heat; stir in 1/3 cup Parmesan cheese. Gradually whisk in eggs until blended.

3 Drain pasta. Add the remaining cheese and butter; toss to coat.

4 Spread a third of the meat mixture in a greased 13-in. x 9-in. baking dish. Layer with half of the pasta, a third of the meat mixture and half of the white sauce. Repeat layers.

5 Bake, uncovered, at 350° for 40-45 minutes or until bubbly.

YIELD: 12 SERVINGS.

greek pasta bake

CAROL STEVENS
BASYE, VIRGINIA

Lemon and herbs complement the cinnamon in this Mediterranean bake.

- 1/2 pound ground beef
- 1/2 pound ground lamb
- 1 large onion, chopped
- 4 garlic cloves, minced
- 3 teaspoons dried oregano
- 1 teaspoon dried basil
- 1/2 teaspoon salt
- 1/4 teaspoon pepper
- 1/4 teaspoon dried thyme
- 1 can (15 ounces) tomato sauce
- 1 can (14-1/2 ounces) diced tomatoes, undrained
- 1 tablespoon lemon juice
- 1 teaspoon sugar
- 1/4 teaspoon ground cinnamon
- 2 cups uncooked rigatoni pasta
- 4 ounces feta cheese, crumbled

1 In a large skillet, cook beef and lamb over medium heat until no longer pink; drain. Stir in the onion, garlic, oregano, basil, salt, pepper and thyme. Add the tomato sauce, tomatoes and lemon juice. Bring to a boil. Reduce heat; simmer, uncovered, for 20 minutes, stirring occasionally.

2 Stir in sugar and cinnamon. Simmer, uncovered, 15 minutes longer.

3 Cook pasta according to package directions; drain. Add to the meat mixture. Transfer mixture to a greased 2-qt. baking dish. Sprinkle with cheese. Cover and bake at 325° for 45 minutes. Uncover; bake 15 minutes longer or until heated through.

YIELD: 6 SERVINGS.

cheeseburger biscuit bake

JOY FRASURE
LONGMONT, COLORADO

Popular cheeseburger ingredients create the tasty layers in this family-pleasing casserole. For the "bun," I use refrigerated biscuits to make a golden topping.

- 1 pound ground beef
- 1/4 cup chopped onion
- 1 can (8 ounces) tomato sauce
- 1/4 cup ketchup
- Dash pepper
- 2 cups (8 ounces) shredded cheddar cheese, *divided*
- 1 tube (12 ounces) refrigerated buttermilk biscuits, separated into 10 biscuits

1 In a large skillet, cook beef and onion over medium heat until meat is no longer pink; drain. Stir in the tomato sauce, ketchup and pepper. Spoon half of mixture into a greased 8-in. square baking dish; sprinkle with half of the cheese. Repeat layers.

2 Place biscuits around edges of dish. Bake, uncovered, at 400° for 18-22 minutes or until the meat mixture is bubbly and biscuits are golden brown.

YIELD: 5 SERVINGS.

crab 'n' penne casserole

BERNADETTE BENNETT
WACO, TEXAS

Purchased Alfredo sauce lends creaminess to this crab casserole, while red pepper flakes kick up the taste. Summer squash and zucchini bring garden-fresh goodness to this comforting main dish.

- 1-1/2 cups uncooked penne pasta
- 1 jar (15 ounces) Alfredo sauce
- 1-1/2 cups imitation crabmeat, chopped
- 1 medium yellow summer squash, sliced
- 1 medium zucchini, sliced
- 1 tablespoon dried parsley flakes
- 1/8 to 1/4 teaspoon crushed red pepper flakes
- 1-1/2 cups (6 ounces) shredded part-skim mozzarella cheese
- 2 tablespoons dry bread crumbs
- 2 teaspoons butter, melted

1 Cook pasta according to package directions. Meanwhile, in a large bowl, combine the Alfredo sauce, crab, yellow squash, zucchini, parsley and pepper flakes. Drain pasta; add to sauce mixture and toss to coat.

2 Transfer to a greased 13-in. x 9-in. baking dish. Sprinkle with cheese. Cover and bake at 325° for 35 minutes or until heated through.

3 Toss bread crumbs and butter; sprinkle over casserole. Bake, uncovered, 5-6 minutes longer or until browned.

YIELD: 6 SERVINGS.

CRAB AND TWIST BAKE: Substitute spiral pasta for the penne and provolone cheese for the mozzarella.

cheddar turkey bake

CAROL DILCHER
EMMAUS, PENNSYLVANIA

This recipe makes two creamy casseroles, so you can serve one for dinner and freeze the second for a night when you're racing the clock.

- 2 cups water
- 2 cups chicken broth
- 4 teaspoons dried minced onion
- 2 cups uncooked long grain rice
- 4 cups cubed cooked turkey
- 2 cups frozen peas, thawed
- 2 cans (10-3/4 ounces *each*) condensed cheddar cheese soup, undiluted
- 2 cups milk
- 1 teaspoon salt
- 2 cups finely crushed butter-flavored crackers (about 60 crackers)
- 6 tablespoons butter, melted

1 In a large saucepan, bring the water, broth and onion to a boil. Reduce heat. Add rice; cover and simmer for 15 minutes or until tender. Remove from the heat; fluff with a fork.

2 Divide rice between two greased 9-in. square baking pans. Sprinkle with turkey and peas. In a large bowl, combine the soup, milk and salt; pour over turkey. Toss the cracker crumbs and butter; sprinkle over the top.

3 Cover and freeze one casserole for up to 3 months. Bake the second casserole, uncovered, at 350° for 35 minutes or until golden brown.

4 **To use frozen casserole:** Thaw in the refrigerator for 24 hours. Bake, uncovered, at 350° for 45-50 minutes or until heated through.

YIELD: 2 CASSEROLES (4-6 SERVINGS EACH).

speedy sweet potatoes

BETH BUHLER
LAWRENCE, KANSAS

I discovered this yummy sweet potato recipe years ago. There's no need for lots of butter and sugar because the pineapple and marshmallows provide plenty of sweetness. It's a perennial favorite at our house.

- 2 cans (15-3/4 ounces *each*) sweet potatoes, drained
- 1/2 teaspoon salt
- 1 can (8 ounces) crushed pineapple, drained
- 1/4 cup coarsely chopped pecans
- 1 tablespoon brown sugar
- 1 cup miniature marshmallows, *divided*

Ground nutmeg

1 In a 1-1/2-qt. microwave-safe dish, layer sweet potatoes, salt, pineapple, pecans, brown sugar and 1/2 cup marshmallows. Cover and microwave on high for 3 to 6 minutes or until bubbly around the edges. Top with the remaining marshmallows.

2 Microwave, uncovered, on high for 1-2 minutes or until marshmallows puff. Sprinkle with nutmeg.

YIELD: 6 SERVINGS.

EDITOR'S NOTE: This recipe was tested in a 1,100-watt microwave.

corn and broccoli bake

BETTY KAY SITZMAN
WRAY, COLORADO

This sweet, comforting side dish is a very creamy casserole that resembles corn pudding. I especially like that it doesn't require a lot of ingredients.

- 1 can (16 ounces) cream-style corn
- 3 cups frozen chopped broccoli, thawed
- 1/2 cup crushed saltines, *divided*
- 1 egg, lightly beaten
- 1 tablespoon dried minced onion

Dash pepper

- 2 tablespoons butter, melted

1 In a large bowl, combine the corn, broccoli, 1/4 cup of saltines, egg, onion and pepper.

2 Place in a greased 1-1/2-qt. baking dish. Combine butter and remaining saltines; sprinkle on top. Cover and bake at 350° for 45 minutes or until a thermometer reads 160°.

YIELD: 6 SERVINGS.

a pinch & a dash

A pinch is approximately the amount of a dry ingredient that can be held between your thumb and forefinger. A dash is a very small amount of seasoning added with a quick downward stroke of the hand. When your grandmother used a dash of an ingredient, she used somewhere between 1/16 and a scant 1/8 teaspoon. If you're re-creating her recipes, you might have to experiment with amounts to get the same results.

TASTE OF HOME TEST KITCHEN

brussels sprouts in wine sauce

STELLA SARGENT
ALEXANDRIA, VIRGINIA

Of all my favorite holiday side dishes, this one stands above the rest. The wine sauce adds a lovely, rich flavor that makes every bite divine.

- 1 package (16 ounces) frozen brussels sprouts
- 1/4 cup butter, cubed
- 1/4 cup all-purpose flour
- 1/2 teaspoon salt
- 1/4 teaspoon pepper
- 1 cup half-and-half cream
- 2/3 cup white wine *or* chicken broth
- 1 jar (16 ounces) whole onions, drained
- 2 tablespoons chopped almonds
- 1 tablespoon minced fresh parsley
- 1 tablespoon sliced almonds

1 Place brussels sprouts and a small amount of water in a microwave-safe dish. Cover and microwave on high for 2 minutes. Stir; microwave 1-2 minutes longer or until partially cooked. Let stand 5 minutes; drain and set aside.

2 In a large saucepan, melt the butter. Stir in the flour, salt and pepper until smooth. Combine the cream and wine. Gradually whisk into flour mixture. Bring to a boil. Cook and stir for 1-2 minutes or until thickened and bubbly. Stir in the onions, chopped almonds, parsley and reserved brussels sprouts.

3 Transfer to a greased 1-1/2-qt. baking dish. Sprinkle with sliced almonds. Bake, uncovered, at 400° for 20-25 minutes or until bubbly and brussels sprouts are tender.

YIELD: 6 SERVINGS.

EDITOR'S NOTE: This recipe was tested in a 1,100-watt microwave.

potato dumpling casserole

JOE ELLEN MESKIMEN
CEDAR RAPIDS, IOWA

This comforting casserole is an impressive side dish for any menu.

DUMPLINGS:

- 2 cups hot mashed potatoes (without milk or seasonings)
- 1 cup all-purpose flour
- 2 eggs, lightly beaten
- 1-1/2 teaspoons salt
- 1/8 teaspoon white pepper
- 1/8 teaspoon ground nutmeg

SAUCE:

- 1 small onion, finely chopped
- 3 tablespoons butter
- 2 tablespoons all-purpose flour
- 1 cup half-and-half cream
- 1 cup chicken broth
- 1/2 cup shredded Swiss cheese, *divided*
- 1/2 cup grated Parmesan cheese, *divided*

Minced fresh parsley, optional

1 Combine all the dumpling ingredients; spoon into a large pastry bag, half at a time, fitted with a large plain tube (opening should be about 1/2 in. diameter). Bring 5 qts. of salted water to a boil in a large stockpot, then adjust heat so water bubbles very gently.

2 Squeeze out the dumplings over simmering water, cutting with scissors at 1-in. intervals and letting the dumplings drop into water. Simmer, uncovered, until the dumplings float, then simmer 1 minute more. Remove with a slotted spoon; drain and keep warm in a 2-qt. baking dish.

3 For the sauce, saute onion in butter until tender. Blend in flour. Add cream and broth all at once. Cook, stirring constantly, until thickened and bubbly.

4 Remove from the heat; stir in 1/4 cup Swiss cheese and 1/4 cup Parmesan cheese. Pour over dumplings; sprinkle with remaining cheese.

5 Bake at 350° for 45 minutes or until hot and bubbly and golden brown on top. Sprinkle with parsley if desired.

YIELD: 8-10 SERVINGS.

EDITOR'S NOTE: Dumplings may also be dropped by teaspoonfuls into boiling water instead of using a pastry bag.

creamy asparagus casserole

JOYCE ALLISON
MILLSAP, TEXAS

My sister created this dish and shared it with me. I always serve it on special holidays. My husband says he hates asparagus, but he loves this casserole!

- 2 pounds fresh asparagus, trimmed, cut into 1-inch pieces
- 1/4 cup butter, cubed
- 1/4 cup all-purpose flour
- 2 cups milk *or* half-and-half cream
- 1/2 teaspoon salt
- 1/4 teaspoon pepper
- 6 hard-cooked eggs, sliced
- 1 cup (4 ounces) shredded cheddar cheese
- 1 cup crushed potato chips

1 In a large saucepan, bring 1/2 in. of water to a boil. Add asparagus; cover and boil for 3 minutes or until crisp-tender. Drain well; set aside.

2 In a large saucepan over medium heat, melt butter. Stir in flour until smooth. Gradually add milk. Bring to a boil over medium heat; cook and stir for 2 minutes or until thickened. Add salt and pepper.

3 In an ungreased 11-in. x 7-in. baking dish, layer half of the asparagus. Cover with half of the eggs, cheese and sauce. Repeat layers. Sprinkle with potato chips.

4 Bake, uncovered, at 350° for 30 minutes or until heated through.

YIELD: 6-8 SERVINGS.

chilies rellenos

IRENE MARTIN
PORTALES, NEW MEXICO

I find that chilies almost always improve a recipe that uses cheese. Sometimes I make this into a main dish by adding shredded cooked chicken after the layer of chilies. It really tastes great!

- 1 can (7 ounces) whole green chilies
- 2 cups (8 ounces) shredded Monterey Jack cheese
- 2 cups (8 ounces) shredded cheddar cheese
- 3 eggs
- 3 cups milk
- 1 cup biscuit/baking mix

Seasoned salt to taste

Salsa

1 Split chilies; rinse and remove seeds. Dry on paper towels. Arrange chilies in an 11-in. x 7-in. baking dish. Top with cheeses.

2 In a large bowl, beat eggs; add milk and biscuit mix. Pour over cheese. Sprinkle with salt. Bake at 325° for 50-55 minutes or until golden brown. Serve with salsa.

YIELD: 8 SERVINGS.

duo tater bake

JOAN MCCULLOCH
ABBOTSFORD, BRITISH COLUMBIA

I made this creamy and comforting potato side dish for Thanksgiving, and it was a winner with my gang. They said to be sure to include it at every holiday dinner. It's a keeper!

- 4 pounds russet *or* Yukon Gold potatoes, peeled and cubed
- 3 pounds sweet potatoes, peeled and cubed
- 2 cartons (8 ounces *each*) spreadable chive and onion cream cheese
- 1 cup (8 ounces) sour cream
- 1/4 cup shredded Colby-Monterey Jack cheese
- 1/3 cup milk
- 1/4 cup shredded Parmesan cheese
- 1/2 teaspoon salt
- 1/2 teaspoon pepper

TOPPING:

- 1 cup (4 ounces) shredded Colby-Monterey Jack cheese
- 1/2 cup chopped green onions
- 1/4 cup shredded Parmesan cheese

1 Place russet potatoes in a Dutch oven and cover with water. Bring to a boil. Reduce heat; cover and cook for 10-15 minutes or until tender.

2 Place sweet potatoes in a large saucepan; cover with water. Bring to a boil. Reduce heat; cover and cook for 10-15 minutes or until tender. Drain; mash with half of cream cheese and sour cream and all of Colby-Monterey Jack cheese.

3 Drain russet potatoes; mash with the remaining cream cheese and sour cream. Stir in the milk, Parmesan cheese, salt and pepper.

4 Spread 2-2/3 cups russet potato mixture into each of two greased 11-in. x 7-in. baking dishes. Layer with 4 cups sweet potato mixture. Repeat layers. Spread with remaining russet potato mixture.

5 Bake, uncovered, at 350° for 15 minutes or until heated through. Combine topping ingredients; sprinkle over casseroles. Bake 2-3 minutes longer or until cheese is melted.

YIELD: 2 CASSEROLES (10 SERVINGS EACH).

tropical sweet potatoes

MARY GAYLORD
BALSAM LAKE, WISCONSIN

Sweet potatoes take on a tropical twist with crushed pineapple mixed in. I add a crumb topping, which bakes to a pretty golden color, and a fresh pineapple garnish.

- 4 large sweet potatoes (3-1/2 pounds)
- 1 can (8 ounces) crushed pineapple, undrained
- 6 tablespoons butter, melted, *divided*
- 3/4 teaspoon salt
- Pinch pepper
- 1/2 cup crushed saltines
- 2 tablespoons brown sugar
- Pinch ground cloves

1 In a large saucepan, cover sweet potatoes with water; bring to a boil. Reduce heat; cover and simmer for 30 minutes or until tender. Drain and cool.

2 Peel the potatoes and place in a large bowl; mash. Add pineapple, 2 tablespoons butter, salt and pepper; mix well.

3 Transfer to a greased 2-qt. baking dish. Combine saltines, brown sugar, cloves and remaining butter; sprinkle over potatoes. Bake, uncovered, at 375° for 30 minutes.

YIELD: 8-10 SERVINGS.

strands with a fork. Combine squash, tomato mixture and all remaining ingredients except Parmesan cheese.

4 Pour into a greased 2-qt. baking dish. Sprinkle with Parmesan cheese. Bake, uncovered, at 375° for 40 minutes or until heated through and top is golden brown.

YIELD: 6 SERVINGS.

vidalia casserole

LIBBY BIGGER
DUNWOODY, GEORGIA

Georgia is famous for the sweet onions grown in the Vidalia area. My family looks forward to the time these onions are available to use in salads and casseroles.

4 to 5 large Vidalia or sweet onions, sliced (1/4 inch thick)
1/4 cup butter
1/4 cup sour cream
3/4 cup grated Parmesan cheese
10 butter-flavored crackers, crushed

1 In a large skillet over medium heat, saute the onions in butter until tender. Remove from the heat; stir in sour cream.

2 Spoon half into a greased 1-qt. baking dish. Sprinkle with cheese. Top with remaining onion mixture and crackers. Bake, uncovered, at 350° for 20-25 minutes or until golden brown and bubbly.

YIELD: 4-6 SERVINGS.

spaghetti squash casserole

GLENAFA VRCHOTA
MASON CITY, IOWA

Don't be fooled by this recipe—it only looks complicated. One of our daughters passed it along with squash from her first garden. It's a real treat!

1 medium spaghetti squash (about 8 inches)
1 cup water
1 tablespoon butter
1 cup chopped onion
2 garlic cloves, minced
1/2 pound sliced fresh mushrooms
1 teaspoon dried basil
1/2 teaspoon dried oregano
1/4 teaspoon dried thyme
1/2 teaspoon salt
1/4 teaspoon pepper
2 medium tomatoes, diced
1 cup ricotta cheese
1/4 cup minced fresh parsley
1 cup dry bread crumbs
1/4 cup grated Parmesan cheese

1 Slice the squash in half lengthwise and scoop out the seeds. Place the squash, cut side down, in a baking dish. Add water and cover tightly with foil. Bake at 375° for about 20-30 minutes or until easily pierced with a fork.

2 Meanwhile, melt butter in skillet. Add the onion, garlic, mushrooms, herbs and seasonings; saute until onion is tender. Add the tomatoes; cook until most of the liquid has evaporated. Set aside.

3 Scoop out the squash, separating

SIDE DISHES

CASSEROLES, SLOW COOKER & SOUPS   33

4 Bake, uncovered, at 375° for 25-30 minutes or until golden brown.
YIELD: 4-6 SERVINGS.

country pineapple casserole

MARGARET LINDEMANN
KENVIL, NEW JERSEY

My family enjoyed this dish at a church ham supper, so I asked for the recipe. I've made it for many covered-dish meals since and have received many compliments. It really is delicious.

- 1/2 cup butter, softened
- 2 cups sugar
- 8 eggs
- 2 cans (20 ounces *each*) crushed pineapple, drained
- 3 tablespoons lemon juice
- 10 slices day-old white bread, cubed

1 In a large bowl, cream butter and sugar until light and fluffy. Add the eggs, one at a time, beating well after each addition. Stir in pineapple and lemon juice. Fold in bread cubes.

2 Pour into a greased 13-in. x 9-in. baking dish. Bake, uncovered, at 325° for 35-40 minutes or until a knife inserted near the center comes out clean.

YIELD: 12-16 SERVINGS.

monterey corn bake

IRENE REDICK
TRENTON, ONTARIO

I am happy to share this 50-year-old recipe with others. It came from my mother-in-law, who taught me how to cook. It is one of my family's all-time favorite dishes, yielding enough for a group. Or cut it in half to serve a few.

- 1 medium onion, chopped
- 5 tablespoons butter, *divided*
- 2 cups sliced fresh mushrooms
- 1 medium sweet red pepper, chopped
- 1/2 teaspoon salt
- 1/4 teaspoon pepper
- 1 garlic clove, minced
- 1 package (16 ounces) frozen corn, thawed
- 2 cups (8 ounces) shredded Colby-Monterey Jack cheese
- 2 teaspoons brown sugar
- 1/2 cup dry bread crumbs
- 2 tablespoons minced fresh parsley

1 In a large skillet, saute onion in 2 tablespoons butter until tender. Add the mushrooms, red pepper, salt and pepper; cook and stir for 5 minutes or until vegetables are tender. Add garlic; cook 1 minute longer.

2 In a greased 2-qt. baking dish, layer half of the corn, mushroom mixture, cheese and brown sugar; repeat layers.

3 Melt the remaining butter; toss with bread crumbs and parsley. Sprinkle over casserole.

get thrifty with bread

Good-quality bread that is beginning to dry out is ideal for cooking because it's more sturdy than fresh bread. To avoid waste, freeze your day-old bread until you're ready to use it in a recipe.

TASTE OF HOME TEST KITCHEN

turnip casserole

DORIS HUBERT
EAST KILLINGLY, CONNECTICUT

Turnips are good alone or with other vegetables. Try chopping them to add texture and flavor to your soups and stews.

     4 medium turnips, peeled and cubed
     1 egg, lightly beaten
   1/3 cup sugar
     3 tablespoons butter
   1/2 teaspoon salt
   1/4 teaspoon ground cinnamon

1 Place turnips in a large saucepan and cover with water. Bring to a boil. Reduce heat; cover and cook for 15 minutes or until tender. Drain. Transfer turnips to a bowl and mash. Add the egg, sugar, butter and salt.

2 Transfer to a greased 1-qt. baking dish; sprinkle with cinnamon. Cover and bake at 350° for 20-25 minutes or until a thermometer reads 160°.

YIELD: 4 SERVINGS.

noodle pudding

EILEEN MEYERS
SCOTT TOWNSHIP, PENNSYLVANIA

Whenever I bring this creamy dish to gatherings, it always prompts recipe requests. The surprising sweet taste comes from apricot nectar, and everyone really enjoys the golden buttery topping.

7-1/2 cups uncooked wide egg noodles
     1 package (8 ounces) cream cheese, softened
     6 tablespoons butter, softened
   1/2 cup sugar
     3 eggs
     1 cup 2% milk
     1 cup apricot nectar
TOPPING:
     1 cup cornflake crumbs
   1/2 cup sugar
     6 tablespoons butter, melted
   1/2 teaspoon ground cinnamon

1 Cook noodles according to package directions. Meanwhile, in a large bowl, beat the cream cheese, butter and sugar until smooth. Beat in eggs. Gradually stir in milk and apricot nectar.

2 Drain noodles; place in a large bowl. Add cream cheese mixture and toss to coat. Transfer to a greased 13-in. x 9-in. baking dish.

3 Combine the topping ingredients; sprinkle over noodles. Bake, uncovered, at 350° for 25-30 minutes or until a thermometer reads 160°.

YIELD: 9 SERVINGS.

quick colander cleanup

Before draining noodles or potatoes, spray the sieve or colander with nonstick cooking spray. It makes cleanup a lot faster and easier.

TERRY N., KINGSPORT, TENNESSEE

corn bread casserole

MARGARET MAYES
LA MESA, CALIFORNIA

We live very close to the Mexican border, so recipes featuring corn and green chilies are popular here. This dish has always been a hit whenever I've taken it to a carry-in dinner.

- 2 packages (8-1/2 ounces *each*) corn bread/muffin mix
- 1 can (15-1/4 ounces) whole kernel corn, drained
- 1 can (14-3/4 ounces) cream-style corn
- 1 can (4 ounces) chopped green chilies, drained
- 1 cup (4 ounces) shredded Monterey Jack cheese

1 Prepare corn bread mixes according to package directions. Pour half of the batter into a greased 11-in. x 7-in. baking dish. Combine corn and creamed corn; spread over batter. Top with chilies and cheese. Carefully spread with remaining corn bread batter.

2 Bake, uncovered, at 375° for 25-30 minutes or until a toothpick comes out clean. Serve warm.

YIELD: 12 SERVINGS.

hearty calico bean bake

HEATHER BIEDLER
MARTINSBURG, WEST VIRGINIA

For years, my mother made this savory-sweet bean dish. I was always thrilled when it was on the menu, and now I serve it often to my own family. You can vary the types of beans used if you wish.

- 1 can (16 ounces) pork and beans, undrained
- 1 can (16 ounces) kidney beans, rinsed and drained
- 1 can (16 ounces) chili beans, undrained
- 1 can (15-1/2 ounces) great northern beans, rinsed and drained
- 1 can (14-1/2 ounces) cut wax beans, drained
- 1-1/2 cups packed brown sugar
- 1-1/2 cups cubed fully cooked ham
- 1-1/2 cups cubed cheddar cheese
- 1/2 cup ketchup
- 1 small onion, chopped
- 2 tablespoons Worcestershire sauce

1 In a large bowl, combine all ingredients. Transfer to a greased shallow 3-qt. baking dish.

2 Bake, uncovered, at 350° for 1 hour or until bubbly and heated through.

YIELD: 10 SERVINGS.

saucy green bean bake

JUNE FORMANEK
BELLE PLAINE, IOWA

Here's a different way to serve green beans. It's a nice change of pace from plain vegetables yet doesn't require much work on your part. Keep it in mind the next time your schedule is full and you have to set dinner on the table.

- 1 can (8 ounces) tomato sauce
- 2 tablespoons diced pimientos
- 1 tablespoon prepared mustard
- 1/4 teaspoon salt
- 1/8 teaspoon pepper
- 1 pound fresh *or* frozen cut green beans, cooked
- 1/2 cup chopped onion
- 1/3 cup chopped green pepper
- 1 garlic clove, minced
- 2 tablespoons butter
- 3/4 cup cubed process cheese (Velveeta)

1 In a large bowl, combine the first five ingredients. Add the green beans; toss to coat. Transfer to an ungreased 1-qt. baking dish. Cover and bake at 350° for 20 minutes.

2 Meanwhile, in a large skillet, saute the onion, green pepper and garlic in butter until tender. Sprinkle over beans. Top with cheese. Bake, uncovered, for 3-5 minutes or until cheese is melted.

YIELD: 4-6 SERVINGS.

tomato crouton casserole

NORMA NELSON
PUNTA GORDA, FLORIDA

This baked dish uses lots of delicious tomatoes and seasonings that give it an Italian twist. Every time I serve this, someone asks for the recipe.

- 8 medium tomatoes, peeled and cut into wedges
- 8 slices bread, crusts removed, cubed
- 1/2 cup plus 2 tablespoons butter, melted
- 1 teaspoon salt
- 1 teaspoon dried basil
- 1 teaspoon dried thyme
- 3/4 cup grated Parmesan cheese

1 Arrange tomatoes in a greased 13-in. x 9-in. baking dish. Top with bread cubes. Combine the butter, salt, basil and thyme; drizzle over bread and tomatoes. Sprinkle with cheese.

2 Bake, uncovered, at 350° for 30-35 minutes or until tomatoes are tender.

YIELD: 8-10 SERVINGS.

customize your green bean casserole

Like many people, I start my green bean casserole with canned cream of mushroom soup. But to spice things up, I add a little horseradish to the sauce. Shredded cheddar cheese on top makes it look scrumptious!

OLIVE S., HAYDENVILLE, MASSACHUSETTS

slow cooker

« MELT-IN-YOUR-MOUTH CHUCK ROAST, P. 66

apple cranberry cider

KATHY WELLS | BRODHEAD, WISCONSIN

Buffets are the best way to feed a crowd. Make this cider ahead, then keep it warm in a slow cooker.

- 3 cinnamon sticks (3 inches), broken
- 1 teaspoon whole cloves
- 2 quarts apple cider *or* juice
- 3 cups cranberry juice
- 2 tablespoons brown sugar

1 Place cinnamon sticks and cloves on a double thickness of cheesecloth; bring up corners of cloth and tie with string to form a bag. In a 5-qt. slow cooker, combine the cider, cranberry juice and brown sugar; add spice bag.

2 Cover and cook on high for 2 hours or until cider reaches desired temperature. Discard spice bag.

YIELD: 11 CUPS.

all-day meatballs

CATHY RYAN | RED WING, MINNESOTA

You can pop these meatballs into the slow cooker the morning of your party, and by the time you're ready, they will be, too!

- 1 cup milk
- 3/4 cup quick-cooking oats
- 3 tablespoons finely chopped onion
- 1-1/2 teaspoons salt
- 1-1/2 pounds ground beef
- 1 cup ketchup
- 1/2 cup water
- 3 tablespoons cider vinegar
- 2 tablespoons sugar

1 In a large bowl, combine the first four ingredients. Crumble beef over mixture and mix well. Shape into 1-in. balls. Place in a 5-qt. slow cooker.

2 In a small bowl, combine the ketchup, water, vinegar and sugar. Pour over the meatballs. Cover and cook on low for 6-8 hours or until the meat is no longer pink.

YIELD: 6 SERVINGS.

make a lot of meatballs

Preparing meatballs in bulk cuts back greatly on prep time. I often make as many as five dinners' worth of meatballs in one evening. To serve, I drop a package of frozen cooked meatballs into simmering spaghetti sauce and heat through. CHRISTI G., TULSA, OKLAHOMA

mexican fondue

NELLA PARKER | HERSEY, MICHIGAN

A handful of items and a few moments of prep work are all you'll need for this festive fondue.

- 1 can (14-3/4 ounces) cream-style corn
- 1 can (14-1/2 ounces) diced tomatoes, drained
- 3 tablespoons chopped green chilies
- 1 teaspoon chili powder
- 1 package (16 ounces) process cheese (Velveeta), cubed

French bread cubes

1 In a small bowl, combine the corn, tomatoes, green chilies and chili powder. Stir in cheese.

2 Spray a 1-1/2-qt. slow cooker with cooking spray. Add corn mixture; cover and cook on high for 1-1/2 hours, stirring every 30 minutes or until cheese is melted. Serve warm with bread cubes.

YIELD: 4-1/2 CUPS.

hot bacon cheese dip

SUZANNE WHITAKER
KNOXVILLE, TENNESSEE

I've tried several appetizer recipes before, but this one is a surefire people-pleaser. The thick dip has lots of bacon flavor.

- 2 packages (8 ounces *each*) cream cheese, cubed
- 4 cups (16 ounces) shredded cheddar cheese
- 1 cup half-and-half cream
- 2 teaspoons Worcestershire sauce
- 1 teaspoon *each* dried minced onion and prepared mustard
- 16 bacon strips, cooked and crumbled

Tortilla chips *or* French bread slices

1 In a 1-1/2-qt. slow cooker, combine the first six ingredients. Cover; cook for 2 hours or until cheeses are melted, stirring occasionally. Just before serving, stir in bacon. Serve warm with tortilla chips or bread.

YIELD: 4 CUPS.

no half-and-half?

For dishes that are cooked or baked, you may substitute 4-1/2 teaspoons melted butter plus enough whole milk to equal 1 cup half-and-half cream. You can also substitute one cup of evaporated milk for each cup of half-and-half cream.

TASTE OF HOME TEST KITCHEN

secret's in the sauce bbq ribs

TANYA REID
WINSTON-SALEM, NORTH CAROLINA

A sweet, rich sauce makes these ribs so tender that the meat literally falls off the bones. And the aroma is wonderful. Yum!

2   racks pork baby back ribs
    (about 4-1/2 pounds)
1-1/2 teaspoons pepper
2-1/2 cups barbecue sauce
3/4 cup cherry preserves
1   tablespoon Dijon mustard
1   garlic clove, minced

1 Cut the ribs into serving-size pieces; sprinkle with pepper. Place in a 5- or 6-qt. slow cooker. Combine remaining ingredients; pour over meat. Cover and cook on low for 6-8 hours or until meat is tender. Serve with sauce.

YIELD: 5 SERVINGS.

slow cook & save money

One of the advantages of preparing food in a slow cooker is that slow cookers use very little electricity because of their low wattage. We contacted our local utility company and found that it would cost less than 50 cents to operate a slow cooker for a total of 10 hours! (This is substantially less than it costs to cook the same food in an oven.) Multiply the low cooking costs for a slow cooker over an entire year, and you will see real savings.

TASTE OF HOME TEST KITCHEN

butterscotch dip

JEAUNE HADL VAN METER
LEXINGTON, KENTUCKY

If you like the sweetness of butterscotch chips, you'll enjoy this warm rum-flavored fruit dip. I serve it with apple and pear wedges. It holds for up to 2 hours in the slow cooker.

  2 packages (10 to 11 ounces *each*) butterscotch chips
2/3 cup evaporated milk
2/3 cup chopped pecans
  1 tablespoon rum extract
Apple and pear wedges

1 In a 1-1/2-qt. slow cooker, combine butterscotch chips and milk. Cover and cook on low for 45-50 minutes or until chips are softened; stir until smooth. Stir in pecans and extract. Serve warm with fruit.

YIELD: ABOUT 3 CUPS.

viennese coffee

SHARON DELANEY-CHRONIS
SOUTH MILWAUKEE, WISCONSIN

This isn't your regular cup of joe! I dress it up with chocolate, whipped cream and more, making it a drink to savor!

  3 cups strong brewed coffee
  3 tablespoons chocolate syrup
  1 teaspoon sugar
1/3 cup heavy whipping cream
1/4 cup creme de cacao *or* Irish cream liqueur
Whipped cream and chocolate curls, optional

1 In a 1-1/2-qt. slow cooker, combine the coffee, chocolate syrup and sugar. Cover and cook on low for 2-1/2 hours.

2 Stir in heavy cream and creme de cacao. Cover and cook 30 minutes longer or until heated through.

3 Ladle the coffee into mugs. Garnish with whipped cream and chocolate curls if desired.

YIELD: 4 SERVINGS.

party meatballs

DEBBIE PAULSEN
APOLLO BEACH, FLORIDA

Meatballs are always great for parties and are so simple to make.

- 1 package (32 ounces) frozen fully cooked homestyle meatballs, thawed
- 1 bottle (14 ounces) ketchup
- 1/4 cup A.1. steak sauce
- 1 tablespoon minced garlic
- 1 teaspoon Dijon mustard

1 Place meatballs in a 3-qt. slow cooker. In a bowl, combine ketchup, steak sauce, garlic and mustard. Pour over meatballs.

2 Cover; cook on low for 3-4 hours or until meatballs are heated through.

YIELD: ABOUT 6 DOZEN.

appetizer ease

For an appetizer buffet that serves as the meal, offer five or six different appetizers (including some substantial selections), and plan on roughly eight pieces per guest. If you'll also be serving a meal, two to three pieces per person is sufficient. Provide a balance of hearty and low-calorie appetizers as well as hot and cold choices. To save time, look for appetizers that can be made ahead and require little last-minute fuss. TASTE OF HOME TEST KITCHEN

peachy spiced cider

ROSE HARMAN | HAYS, KANSAS

I served this spiced cider at a get-together and received so many compliments. Everyone enjoys the subtle peach flavor.

- 4 cans (5-1/2 ounces *each*) peach nectar *or* apricot nectar
- 2 cups apple juice
- 1/4 to 1/2 teaspoon ground ginger
- 1/4 teaspoon ground cinnamon
- 1/4 teaspoon ground nutmeg
- 4 fresh orange slices (1/4 inch thick), halved

1 In a 1-1/2-qt. slow cooker, combine the first five ingredients. Top with the orange slices. Cover and cook on low for 4-6 hours or until heated through. Stir before serving.

YIELD: ABOUT 1 QUART.

hot cranberry punch

LAURA BURGESS | BALLWIN, MISSOURI

I serve this rosy spiced beverage at winter gatherings. Friends like the zesty twist it gets from the red-hot candies.

       8 cups hot water
 1-1/2 cups sugar
       4 cups cranberry juice
   3/4 cup orange juice
   1/4 cup lemon juice
      12 whole cloves, optional
   1/2 cup red-hot candies

1 In a 5-qt. slow cooker, combine water, sugar and juices; stir until sugar is dissolved. If desired, place cloves in a double thickness of cheesecloth; bring up corners of cloth and tie with string to form a bag. Add spice bag and red-hot candies to slow cooker.

2 Cover and cook on low for 2-3 hours or until heated through. Before serving, discard the spice bag and stir the punch.

YIELD: 3-1/2 QUARTS.

slow cooker mexican dip

HEATHER COURTNEY | AMES, IOWA

We love to entertain, and this satisfying seven-ingredient dip is always popular. It is easy to put together, and using the slow cooker leaves us free to share some quality time with our guests. After all, isn't that the purpose of a party?

 1-1/2 pounds ground beef
     1 pound bulk hot Italian sausage
     1 cup chopped onion
     1 package (8.8 ounces) ready-to-serve Spanish rice
     1 can (16 ounces) refried beans
     1 can (10 ounces) enchilada sauce
     1 pound process cheese (Velveeta), cubed
       Baked tortilla chip scoops

1 In a Dutch oven, cook the beef, sausage and onion over medium heat until meat is no longer pink; drain. Heat rice according to package directions.

2 In a 3-qt. slow cooker, combine the meat mixture, rice, beans, enchilada sauce and cheese. Cover and cook on low for 1-1/2 to 2 hours or until cheese is melted. Serve with tortilla scoops.

YIELD: 8 CUPS.

ginger tea drink

ALEXANDRA MARCOTTY
CLEVELAND HEIGHTS, OHIO

Looking for something new and special to serve? Let this soothing green tea simmer while you concentrate on preparing other dishes for your get-together. Everyone who tries it will ask for the heartwarming recipe.

    4 cups boiling water
   15 individual green tea bags
    4 cups white grape juice
    1 to 2 tablespoons honey
    1 tablespoon minced fresh
       gingerroot
Crystallized ginger, optional

1 In a 3-qt. slow cooker, combine boiling water and tea bags. Cover and let stand for 10 minutes. Discard tea bags. Stir in the remaining ingredients. Cover and cook on low for 2-3 hours or until heated through.

2 Strain if desired before serving warm. Garnish with slices of crystallized ginger if desired.

YIELD: 2 QUARTS.

sweet-and-sour chicken wings

JUNE EBERHARDT
MARYSVILLE, CALIFORNIA

These wings are perfect for gatherings. Because they come with plenty of sauce, I sometimes serve them over rice as a main dish. Any way you do it, this sweet and tangy medley will be a hit!

    1 cup sugar
    1 cup cider vinegar
  1/2 cup ketchup
    2 tablespoons reduced-sodium soy sauce
    1 teaspoon chicken bouillon granules
   16 chicken wings
    6 tablespoons cornstarch
  1/2 cup cold water

1 In a small saucepan, combine the first five ingredients. Bring to a boil; cook and stir until sugar is dissolved. Cut wings into three sections; discard wing tip sections. Transfer to a 3-qt. slow cooker; add vinegar mixture. Cover and cook on low for 3 to 3-1/2 hours or until chicken juices run clear.

2 Transfer wings to a serving dish and keep warm. Skim fat from cooking juices; transfer to a small saucepan. Bring liquid to a boil. Combine cornstarch and water until smooth. Gradually stir into the pan. Bring to a boil; cook and stir for 2 minutes or until thickened. Spoon over chicken. Serve with a slotted spoon.

YIELD: 32 APPETIZERS.

EDITOR'S NOTE: Uncooked chicken wing sections (wingettes) may be substituted for whole chicken wings.

chipotle ham 'n' cheese dip

LISA RENSHAW
KANSAS CITY, MISSOURI

During the busy holiday season, you just can't beat convenient slow cooker recipes like this one that allow you to visit with guests instead of working away in the kitchen.

  2 packages (8 ounces *each*) cream cheese, cubed
  1 can (12 ounces) evaporated milk
  8 ounces Gouda cheese, shredded
  1 cup (4 ounces) shredded cheddar cheese
  2 tablespoons chopped chipotle pepper in adobo sauce
  1 teaspoon ground cumin
  2 cups diced fully cooked ham
Fresh vegetables *or* tortilla chips

1 In a 3-qt. slow cooker, combine the first six ingredients. Cover and cook on low for 40 minutes.

2 Stir in ham; cook 20 minutes longer or until heated through. Serve warm with vegetables or tortilla chips.

YIELD: 7 CUPS.

mulled merlot

TASTE OF HOME TEST KITCHEN

We created this flavor sensation that's sure to warm up friends and family!

  4 cinnamon sticks (3 inches)
  4 whole cloves
  2 bottles (750 milliliters *each*) merlot
1/2 cup sugar
1/2 cup orange juice
1/2 cup brandy
  1 medium orange, thinly sliced

1 Place cinnamon sticks and cloves on a double thickness of cheesecloth; bring up corners of cloth and tie with string to form a bag.

2 In a 3-qt. slow cooker, combine the wine, sugar, orange juice, brandy and orange slices. Add spice bag. Cover and cook on high for 1 hour or until heated through. Discard spice bag and orange slices. Serve the wine warm in mugs.

YIELD: 9 SERVINGS.

green olive dip

BETH DUNAHAY
LIMA, OHIO

Olive fans will love this dip. It's
cheesy and full of beef and beans. It
could even be used to fill taco shells.

1   pound ground beef
1   medium sweet red pepper,
    chopped
1   small onion, chopped
1   can (16 ounces) refried beans
1   jar (16 ounces) mild salsa
2   cups (8 ounces) shredded part-
    skim mozzarella cheese
2   cups (8 ounces) shredded
    cheddar cheese
1   jar (5-3/4 ounces) sliced green
    olives with pimientos, drained
Tortilla chips

1   In a large skillet, cook the beef,
    pepper and onion over medium heat
    until meat is no longer pink; drain.

2   Transfer to a greased 3-qt. slow
    cooker. Add the beans, salsa,
    cheeses and olives. Cover and cook
    on low for 3-4 hours or until cheese
    is melted, stirring occasionally. Serve
    with chips.

YIELD: 8 CUPS.

warm pomegranate punch

TASTE OF HOME TEST KITCHEN

If you're looking for something special to serve on a chilly evening, try this warming punch. It has a subtle tea flavor, and the juices create just the right balance of sweet and tart.

- 4 cups pomegranate juice
- 4 cups unsweetened apple juice
- 2 cups brewed tea
- 1/2 cup sugar
- 1/3 cup lemon juice
- 3 cinnamon sticks (3 inches)
- 12 whole cloves

1 In a 4- or 5-qt. slow cooker, combine the first five ingredients. Place cinnamon sticks and cloves on a double thickness of cheesecloth; bring up corners of cloth and tie with string to form a bag. Add spice bag to slow cooker.

2 Cover and cook on low for 2-4 hours or until heated through. Discard spice bag. Serve warm.

YIELD: 2-1/2 QUARTS.

warm broccoli cheese dip

BARBARA MAIOL
CONYERS, GEORGIA

When my family gathers for a party, this flavorful, creamy dip is served. Everyone loves its zip from the jalapeno pepper and the crunch of the broccoli.

- 2 jars (8 ounces *each*) process cheese sauce
- 1 can (10-3/4 ounces) condensed cream of chicken soup, undiluted
- 3 cups frozen chopped broccoli, thawed and drained
- 1/2 pound fresh mushrooms, chopped
- 2 tablespoons chopped seeded jalapeno pepper

Assorted fresh vegetables

1 In a 1-1/2-qt. slow cooker, combine cheese sauce and soup. Cover and cook on low for 30 minutes or until cheese is melted, stirring occasionally. Stir in the broccoli, mushrooms and jalapeno. Cover and cook on low for 2-3 hours or until vegetables are tender. Serve with assorted fresh vegetables.

YIELD: 5-1/2 CUPS.

EDITOR'S NOTE: We recommend wearing disposable gloves when cutting hot peppers. Avoid touching your face.

celery slices

I love to serve those cute little peeled carrots on veggie trays when I'm entertaining. To make the celery look just as nice, I wash the ribs, then cut them on a diagonal into 1-inch slices. I find it's quick to do, and my guests comment on how nice the celery looks alongside the baby carrots.

ARDIS B., GLENCOE, MINNESOTA

sausage pepper sandwiches

SUZETTE GESSEL
ALBUQUERQUE, NEW MEXICO

Peppers and onions add a fresh taste to this zippy sausage filling for sandwiches. My mother gave me this recipe.

> 6 Italian sausage links (4 ounces *each*)
> 1 medium green pepper, cut into 1-inch pieces
> 1 large onion, cut into 1-inch pieces
> 1 can (8 ounces) tomato sauce
> 1/8 teaspoon pepper
> 6 hoagie *or* submarine sandwich buns, split

1 In a large skillet, brown sausage links over medium heat. Cut into 1/2-in. slices; place in a 3-qt. slow cooker. Stir in the green pepper, onion, tomato sauce and pepper.

2 Cover and cook on low for 7-8 hours or until sausage is no longer pink and vegetables are tender. Use a slotted spoon to serve on buns.

YIELD: 6 SERVINGS.

meat loaf burgers

PEGGY BURDICK
BURLINGTON, MICHIGAN

These hearty bites are great for potlucks. Served on hamburger buns, the patties get a flavor boost when topped with the seasoned tomato sauce.

> 1 large onion, sliced
> 1 celery rib, chopped
> 2 pounds lean ground beef (90% lean)
> 1-1/2 teaspoons salt, *divided*
> 1/4 teaspoon pepper
> 2 cups tomato juice
> 4 garlic cloves, minced
> 1 tablespoon ketchup
> 1 teaspoon Italian seasoning
> 1 bay leaf
> 6 hamburger buns, split

1 Place onion and celery in a 3-qt. slow cooker. Combine beef, 1 teaspoon salt and pepper; shape into six patties. Place over onion mixture. Combine the tomato juice, garlic, ketchup, Italian seasoning, bay leaf and remaining salt. Pour over the patties.

2 Cover and cook on low for 7-9 hours or until meat is tender. Discard bay leaf. Separate patties with a spatula if necessary; serve on buns.

YIELD: 6 SERVINGS.

better meat loaf

If your favorite meat loaf recipe calls for ketchup or tomato sauce, try substituting spaghetti sauce. You'll be pleasantly surprised.

MARGIE S., MONROEVILLE, PENNSYLVANIA

bavarian meatballs

PEGGY RIOS
MECHANICSVILLE, VIRGINIA

I use my slow cooker often, and these mouthwatering meatballs are just one reason why. They're a guaranteed crowd-pleaser when I serve them as party appetizers—or a yummy sandwich spooned over crusty rolls and topped with cheese.

- 1 package (32 ounces) frozen fully cooked Italian meatballs
- 1/2 cup chopped onion
- 1/4 cup packed brown sugar
- 1 envelope onion soup mix
- 1 can (12 ounces) beer *or* nonalcoholic beer
- 12 hoagie buns, split
- 3 cups (12 ounces) shredded Swiss cheese

1 In a 3-qt. slow cooker, combine the meatballs, onion, brown sugar, soup mix and beer.

2 Cover and cook on low for 3-1/2 to 4-1/2 hours or until heated through.

3 Serve with toothpicks for an appetizer. Or for sandwiches, place six meatballs on each bun bottom. Sprinkle each sandwich with 1/4 cup cheese. Place on baking sheets.

4 Broil 4-6 in. from the heat for 2-3 minutes or until cheese is melted. Replace bun tops.

YIELD: 12 SERVINGS.

shredded venison sandwiches

RUTH SETTERLUND
FREYBURG, MAINE

My husband hunts for deer every November, so I'm always looking for new recipes for venison. The whole family loves these slow cooker sandwiches.

- 1 boneless venison roast (4 pounds)
- 1-1/2 cups ketchup
- 3 tablespoons brown sugar
- 1 tablespoon ground mustard
- 1 tablespoon lemon juice
- 1 tablespoon soy sauce
- 1 tablespoon Liquid Smoke, optional
- 2 teaspoons *each* celery salt, pepper and Worcestershire sauce
- 1 teaspoon *each* onion powder and garlic powder
- 1/8 teaspoon ground nutmeg
- 3 drops hot pepper sauce
- 14 to 18 hamburger buns, split

1 Cut venison roast in half; place in a 5-qt. slow cooker. In a large bowl, combine the ketchup, brown sugar, mustard, lemon juice, soy sauce, Liquid Smoke if desired and seasonings. Pour over venison. Cover and cook on high for 4-1/2 to 5 hours or until meat is tender.

2 Remove the roast; set aside to cool. Strain sauce and return to slow cooker. Shred meat with two forks; return to the slow cooker and heat through. Using a slotted spoon, spoon meat mixture onto each bun.

YIELD: 14-18 SERVINGS.

hearty italian sandwiches

ELAINE KRUPSKY
LAS VEGAS, NEVADA

I've made this sweet and spicy sandwich filling for many years. It tastes as good as it smells!

1-1/2 pounds lean ground beef (90% lean)
1-1/2 pounds bulk Italian sausage
2 large onions, sliced
2 large green peppers, sliced
2 large sweet red peppers, sliced
1 teaspoon *each* salt and pepper
1/4 teaspoon crushed red pepper flakes
8 sandwich rolls, split
Shredded Monterey Jack cheese, optional

1 In a Dutch oven, cook beef and sausage over medium heat until no longer pink; drain. Place a third of the onions and peppers in a 5-qt. slow cooker; top with half of the meat mixture. Repeat layers; top with remaining vegetables. Sprinkle with salt, pepper and pepper flakes.

2 Cover; cook on low for 6 hours or until vegetables are tender. With a slotted spoon, serve about 1 cup of meat and vegetables on each roll. Top with cheese if desired. Use pan juices for dipping if desired.

YIELD: 8 SERVINGS.

barbecue beef sandwiches

JAN WALLS
DOVER, DELAWARE

I work for the Delaware Department of Transportation and prepare this simple dish during storm emergencies and for luncheon get-togethers.

1 teaspoon celery salt
1 teaspoon garlic powder
1 teaspoon onion powder
1 fresh beef brisket (3 to 5 pounds), halved
3 tablespoons Liquid Smoke, optional
1 tablespoon hot pepper sauce
1 bottle (18 ounces) barbecue sauce
12 sandwich rolls, split

1 Combine the celery salt, garlic powder and onion powder; rub over brisket. Place in a 5-qt. slow cooker. Combine Liquid Smoke if desired and hot pepper sauce; pour over brisket. Cover and cook on low for 6-8 hours or until the meat is tender.

2 Remove roast and cool slightly. Strain cooking juices, reserving 1/2 cup. Shred meat with two forks; place in a large saucepan. Add the barbecue sauce and reserved cooking juices; heat through. Serve about 1/3 cup meat mixture on each roll.

YIELD: 12 SERVINGS.

EDITOR'S NOTE: This is a fresh beef brisket, not corned beef.

freeze veggies

Freezing peppers and onions is a great way to enjoy garden produce. A medium green pepper, chopped, will yield about 1 cup. A large green pepper, chopped, will yield about 1-1/3 to 1-1/2 cups. A medium onion, chopped, will equal about 1/2 cup; a large onion will yield about 1 cup. Store both green peppers and onions in heavy-duty resealable plastic bags. Green peppers can be frozen for up to 6 months, and onions can be frozen for up to 1 year.

TASTE OF HOME TEST KITCHEN

pulled pork sandwiches

TIFFANY MARTINEZ
ALISO VIEJO, CALIFORNIA

Preparing pork roast in the slow cooker makes it moist and tender, so it's just ideal for these sandwiches. The meat shreds nicely, and the cumin and garlic add just the right flavor. The sourdough bread, chipotle mayonnaise, cheese and tomato make it complete.

- 1 boneless pork sirloin roast (2 pounds), trimmed
- 1 cup barbecue sauce
- 1/4 cup chopped onion
- 2 garlic cloves, minced
- 1/2 teaspoon ground cumin
- 1/4 teaspoon salt
- 1/8 teaspoon pepper
- 16 slices sourdough bread
- 1 chipotle pepper in adobo sauce, chopped
- 3/4 cup mayonnaise
- 8 slices cheddar cheese
- 2 plum tomatoes, thinly sliced

1 Place pork in a 3-qt. slow cooker. Combine the barbecue sauce, onion, garlic, cumin, salt and pepper; pour over pork. Cover and cook on low for 6-7 hours or until meat is tender. Remove meat. Shred with two forks and return to slow cooker; heat through.

2 Place bread on an ungreased baking sheet. Broil 4-6 in. from the heat for 2-3 minutes on each side or until golden brown.

3 Meanwhile, in a small bowl, combine chipotle pepper and mayonnaise; spread over toast. Spoon 1/2 cup meat mixture onto each of eight slices of toast. Top with cheese, tomatoes and remaining toast.

YIELD: 8 SERVINGS.

slow cooker sloppy joes

CAROL LOSIER
BALDWINSVILLE, NEW YORK

This is perfect for hot summer days when you want something hearty that doesn't heat up the kitchen! It's easy to double or triple for crowds, and if there are any leftovers, you can freeze them to enjoy later!

- 1-1/2 pounds ground beef
- 1 cup chopped celery
- 1/2 cup chopped onion
- 1 bottle (12 ounces) chili sauce
- 2 tablespoons brown sugar
- 2 tablespoons sweet pickle relish
- 1 tablespoon Worcestershire sauce
- 1 teaspoon salt
- 1/8 teaspoon pepper
- 8 hamburger buns, split

1 In a large skillet, cook the beef, celery and onion over medium heat until meat is no longer pink; drain. Transfer to a 3-qt. slow cooker.

2 Stir in the chili sauce, brown sugar, pickle relish, Worcestershire sauce, salt and pepper.

3 Cover and cook on low for 3-4 hours or until flavors are combined. Spoon 1/2 cup beef mixture onto each bun.

YIELD: 8 SERVINGS.

hot ham sandwiches

SUSAN REHM
GRAHAMSVILLE, NEW YORK

I came up with this crowd-pleasing recipe when trying to re-create a sandwich I tried at a favorite restaurant near my hometown. The secret ingredient is sweet relish.

        3 pounds thinly sliced deli ham
          (about 40 slices)
        2 cups apple juice
      2/3 cup packed brown sugar
      1/2 cup sweet pickle relish
        2 teaspoons prepared mustard
        1 teaspoon paprika
       12 kaiser rolls, split
Additional sweet pickle relish, optional

1 Separate ham slices and place in a 3-qt. slow cooker. In a small bowl, combine the apple juice, brown sugar, relish, mustard and paprika. Pour over ham.

2 Cover and cook on low for 4-5 hours or until heated through. Place 3-4 slices of ham on each roll. Serve with additional relish if desired.

YIELD: 12 SERVINGS.

shredded beef sandwiches

BUNNY PALMERTREE
CARROLLTON, MISSISSIPPI

I like to serve these tasty handhelds with a no-fuss side of crunchy coleslaw. The homemade barbecue sauce is exceptional and wonderful for dipping!

        1 can (10-1/2 ounces)
          condensed beef broth, undiluted
        1 cup ketchup
      1/2 cup packed brown sugar
      1/2 cup lemon juice
        3 tablespoons steak sauce
        2 garlic cloves, minced
        1 teaspoon pepper
        1 teaspoon Worcestershire sauce
        1 beef eye round roast
          (3-1/2 pounds), cut in half
        1 teaspoon salt
       16 sandwich buns, split
Dill pickle slices, optional

1 In a small bowl, whisk the first eight ingredients. Pour half of mixture into a 5-qt. slow cooker. Sprinkle beef with salt; add to slow cooker and top with remaining broth mixture.

2 Cover and cook on low for 10-12 hours or until meat is tender. Shred meat with two forks and return to slow cooker. Using a slotted spoon, place 1/2 cup beef mixture on each bun. Top with pickles if desired.

YIELD: 16 SERVINGS.

italian sausage hoagies

CRAIG WACHS
RACINE, WISCONSIN

In southeastern Wisconsin, our cuisine is influenced by our German and Italian heritage. We often use German bratwurst for the Italian sausage in this recipe to blend the two cultural influences.

10   Italian sausage links
 2   tablespoons olive oil
 1   jar (26 ounces) meatless spaghetti sauce
1/2 medium green pepper, julienned
1/2 medium sweet red pepper, julienned
1/2 cup water
1/4 cup grated Romano cheese
 2   tablespoons *each* dried oregano and dried basil
 2   loaves French bread (20 inches)

1 In a large skillet over medium-high heat, brown sausage in oil; drain. Transfer to a 5-qt. slow cooker. Add spaghetti sauce, peppers, water, cheese and spices. Cover; cook on low for 4 hours or until sausage is no longer pink.

2 Slice each French bread loaf lengthwise but not all the way through; cut each loaf widthwise into five pieces. Fill each with sausage, peppers and sauce.

YIELD: 10 SERVINGS.

olive oil explained

With all the different olive oils on grocery store shelves today, choosing one can be confusing. But it may help to know that olive oils are graded according to acidity. Extra-virgin olive oil is the top grade and is extremely low in acidity (1%). It is produced by the first crushing and pressing of tree-ripened olives and has a deep color and intense olive flavor. Virgin olive oil also comes from the first pressing of olives but has a slightly higher acidity (2%), lighter color and less fruity flavor. Both of these oils are best used in dishes where their flavors can be appreciated.

TASTE OF HOME TEST KITCHEN

fiesta chicken burritos

MARGARET LATTA
PADUCAH, KENTUCKY

Looking for some heat with supper but still want a cool kitchen? Try these slow-cooked burritos with a spicy touch the whole family will love! This is a simple recipe to double if you're feeding a crowd. For those who prefer a spicier dish, increase the cayenne pepper to a full teaspoon.

1-1/2 pounds boneless skinless chicken breasts
1 can (15-1/4 ounces) whole kernel corn, drained
1 can (15 ounces) black beans, rinsed and drained
1 can (10 ounces) diced tomatoes and green chilies, undrained
1 jalapeno pepper, seeded and finely chopped
3 tablespoons ground cumin
1 teaspoon salt
1 teaspoon paprika
1/2 teaspoon pepper
Dash cayenne pepper
Dash crushed red pepper flakes
1 package (8 ounces) reduced-fat cream cheese
8 flour tortillas (8 inches), warmed
Optional toppings: sour cream, shredded cheddar cheese, shredded lettuce and chopped tomatoes

1 Place chicken in a greased 4-qt. slow cooker. In a large bowl, combine the corn, beans, tomatoes, jalapeno and seasonings; pour over chicken. Cover and cook on low for 4-5 hours or until chicken is tender.

2 Remove chicken; cool slightly. Shred meat with two forks and return to the slow cooker. Stir in cream cheese. Cover and cook 15 minutes longer or until heated through.

3 Spoon 3/4 cup chicken mixture down the center of each tortilla; add toppings of your choice. Fold sides and ends over filling and roll up.

YIELD: 8 SERVINGS.

EDITOR'S NOTE : We recommend wearing disposable gloves when cutting hot peppers. Avoid touching your face.

slow-cooked turkey sandwiches

DIANE TWAIT NELSEN
RINGSTED, IOWA

These sandwiches have been such a hit at office potlucks that I keep copies of the recipe in my desk to hand out.

- 6 cups cubed cooked turkey
- 2 cups cubed process cheese (Velveeta)
- 1 can (10-3/4 ounces) condensed cream of chicken soup, undiluted
- 1 can (10-3/4 ounces) condensed cream of mushroom soup, undiluted
- 1/2 cup finely chopped onion
- 1/2 cup chopped celery
- 22 wheat sandwich buns, split

1 In a 3-qt. slow cooker, combine the first six ingredients. Cover and cook on low for 3-4 hours or until onion and celery are tender and cheese is melted. Stir mixture before spooning 1/2 cup onto each bun.

YIELD: 22 SERVINGS.

turkey sloppy joes

NICHOLE JONES
PLEASANT GROVE, UTAH

Chili sauce and turkey make these sloppy joes deliciously unique.

- 1-1/2 pounds lean ground turkey
- 2 medium onions, finely chopped
- 4 garlic cloves, minced
- 1 jar (12 ounces) chili sauce
- 1 jalapeno pepper, seeded and chopped
- 1 tablespoon Worcestershire sauce
- 2 teaspoons dried oregano
- 1 teaspoon ground cumin
- 1 teaspoon paprika
- 1/2 teaspoon salt
- 1/2 teaspoon pepper
- 2 cups (8 ounces) shredded Monterey Jack cheese
- 8 onion rolls, split
- 2 medium ripe avocados, peeled and thinly sliced

1 In a large skillet coated with cooking spray, cook the turkey, onions and garlic over medium heat until meat is no longer pink; drain.

2 Transfer to a 1-1/2-qt. slow cooker. Stir in the chili sauce, jalapeno, Worcestershire sauce, oregano, cumin, paprika, salt and pepper. Cover and cook on low for 4-5 hours or until heated through. Just before serving, stir in cheese. Serve on rolls topped with avocado.

YIELD: 8 SERVINGS.

EDITOR'S NOTE: We recommend wearing disposable gloves when cutting hot peppers. Avoid touching your face.

ground meat

Ground meat is labeled and sold based on the percentage of fat by weight. If you want to purchase lean meat, check the label and look for less than 10% fat by weight. When comparing ground beef to ground turkey or chicken, any package labeled with the same fat percentage will have the same number of calories and total fat grams. For instance, a 1-pound package labeled 91/9 will have 91% lean to 9% fat by weight, regardless of whether the content is beef, turkey or chicken.

TASTE OF HOME TEST KITCHEN

zippy beef fajitas

LAURIE SADOWSKI
ST. CATHARINES, ONTARIO

This is a flavorful and fast way to prepare steak filling for fajitas. The yummy flavor comes from aromatic ingredients like garlic and gingerroot. There's even a can of cola in the recipe.

  1 beef flank steak (1-1/2 pounds)
  2 teaspoons ground ginger
  2 teaspoons crushed red pepper flakes
3/4 teaspoon garlic powder
1/4 teaspoon pepper
  1 medium sweet red pepper, cut into strips
  1 medium green pepper, cut into strips
  1 can (12 ounces) cola
  5 green onions, chopped
1/3 cup soy sauce
  2 tablespoons minced fresh gingerroot
  2 tablespoons tomato paste
  1 garlic clove, minced
  6 flour tortillas (8 inches), warmed

1 Cut steak in half lengthwise. In a small bowl, combine the ground ginger, pepper flakes, garlic powder and pepper; rub over steak. Transfer to a 3-qt. slow cooker; add red and green peppers. Combine the cola, green onions, soy sauce, gingerroot, tomato paste and garlic; pour over top.

2 Cover and cook on low 6-7 hours or until meat is tender.

3 Shred the meat with two forks and return to the slow cooker; heat through. Spoon beef mixture off center onto each tortilla using a slotted spoon. Fold sides over filling.

YIELD: 6 SERVINGS.

brats with sauerkraut

DARLENE DIXON
HANOVER, MINNESOTA

I've made many variations on this excellent main dish. The bratwurst can be plain, smoked or cheese-flavored, served whole or cut in slices, with a bun or without. It would be popular at a party or potluck.

  8 uncooked bratwurst links
  1 can (14 ounces) sauerkraut, rinsed and well drained
  2 medium apples, peeled and finely chopped
  3 bacon strips, cooked and crumbled
1/4 cup packed brown sugar
1/4 cup finely chopped onion
  1 teaspoon ground mustard
  8 brat buns, split

1 Place the bratwurst in a 5-qt. slow cooker. In a large bowl, combine the sauerkraut, apples, bacon, brown sugar, onion and mustard; spoon over bratwurst. Cover and cook on low for 6-7 hours or until the meat is no longer pink.

2 Place brats in buns; using a slotted spoon, top with sauerkraut mixture.

YIELD: 8 SERVINGS.

ham barbecue

JENNIFER MIDDLEKAUFF
NEW HOLLAND, PENNSYLVANIA

We have used this recipe countless times for family gatherings and birthday parties. The sandwiches are so easy to make, and they taste great. In fact, I usually double the recipe so I'm sure to have leftovers.

        2 pounds thinly sliced deli ham
        1 cup water
        1 cup ketchup
      1/4 cup packed brown sugar
      1/4 cup Worcestershire sauce
        2 tablespoons white vinegar
        2 teaspoons prepared mustard
       12 hamburger buns, split and toasted

1 Place the ham in a greased 3-qt. slow cooker. In a large bowl, combine the water, ketchup, brown sugar, Worcestershire sauce, vinegar and mustard; pour over ham and stir well. Cover and cook on low for 4-5 hours or until heated through. Serve on hamburger buns.

YIELD: 12 SERVINGS.

shredded steak sandwiches

LEE DENEAU
LANSING, MICHIGAN

I received this recipe when I was a newlywed, and it's been a favorite since then. The saucy steak barbecue makes a quick meal served on sliced buns or even over rice, potatoes or buttered noodles.

        3 pounds beef top round steak, cut into large pieces
        2 large onions, chopped
      3/4 cup thinly sliced celery
    1-1/2 cups ketchup
      1/2 to 3/4 cup water
      1/3 cup lemon juice
      1/3 cup Worcestershire sauce
        3 tablespoons brown sugar
        3 tablespoons cider vinegar
        2 to 3 teaspoons salt
        2 teaspoons prepared mustard
    1-1/2 teaspoons paprika
        1 teaspoon chili powder
      1/2 teaspoon pepper
      1/8 to 1/4 teaspoon hot pepper sauce
       12 to 14 sandwich rolls, split

1 Place meat in a 5-qt. slow cooker. Add onions and celery. In a bowl, combine the ketchup, water, lemon juice, Worcestershire sauce, brown sugar, vinegar, salt, mustard, paprika, chili powder, pepper and hot pepper sauce. Pour over meat.

2 Cover and cook on high for 6-8 hours or until meat is tender. Remove meat; cool slightly. Shred with two forks. Return to slow cooker and heat through. Serve on rolls.

YIELD: 12-14 SERVINGS.

shredding meat for sandwiches

Remove cooked meat from the slow cooker with a slotted spoon and allow it to cool slightly for easier handling. Place meat in a shallow pan. With two forks, pull meat into thin shreds. Return shredded meat to the slow cooker to heat through.

sesame
orange chicken

DARLENE BRENDEN
SALEM, OREGON

The enticing aroma of oranges and barbecue greets you when you remove the lid from this tasty dish. This is a hot, hearty meal you can enjoy any time of the year.

- 1/2 cup all-purpose flour
- 4 pounds boneless skinless chicken thighs
- 2/3 cup teriyaki sesame ginger barbecue sauce
- 2/3 cup orange marmalade
- 1/2 cup orange juice
- 1/4 cup soy sauce
- 1 tablespoon minced fresh gingerroot
- 1/2 teaspoon crushed red pepper flakes
- 2 tablespoons sesame seeds, toasted

Hot cooked rice

toasting
sesame seeds

Toast sesame seeds in a dry skillet over medium heat for 3-5 minutes or until lightly browned, stirring occasionally. Or bake on an ungreased baking sheet at 350° for 8-10 minutes.

TASTE OF HOME TEST KITCHEN

1 Place flour in a large resealable plastic bag. Add the chicken, a few pieces at a time, and shake to coat. Transfer to a 4- or 5-qt. slow cooker.

2 In a large bowl, combine the barbecue sauce, marmalade, orange juice, soy sauce, ginger and pepper flakes. Pour over chicken. Cover and cook on low for 4-6 hours or until meat is tender. Sprinkle with sesame seeds. Serve with rice.

YIELD: 8 SERVINGS.

cornish hens
with potatoes

DEBORAH RANDALL
ABBEVILLE, LOUISIANA

This is a wonderful meal that takes very little work but is special enough for company. I serve it with green beans and French bread.

- 4 Cornish game hens (20 to 24 ounces *each*)
- 2 tablespoons canola oil
- 4 large red potatoes, cut into 1/8-inch slices
- 4 bacon strips, cut into 1-inch pieces

Lemon-pepper seasoning and garlic powder to taste

Minced fresh parsley

1 In a large skillet, brown hens in oil. Place the potatoes in a 5-qt. slow cooker. Top with the hens and bacon. Sprinkle with lemon-pepper and garlic powder.

2 Cover and cook on low for 6-8 hours or until a meat thermometer reads 180° and potatoes are tender. Thicken the cooking juices if desired. Sprinkle the hens with parsley.

YIELD: 4 SERVINGS.

vegetarian stuffed peppers

MELISSA MCCABE
LONG BEACH, CALIFORNIA

These filling and flavorful peppers are an updated version of my mom's stuffed peppers, which were a favorite when I was growing up in upstate New York. Whenever I make them, I'm reminded of home.

- 6 large sweet peppers
- 2 cups cooked brown rice
- 3 small tomatoes, chopped
- 1 cup frozen corn, thawed
- 1 small sweet onion, chopped
- 1/3 cup canned red beans, rinsed and drained
- 1/3 cup canned black beans, rinsed and drained
- 3/4 cup cubed Monterey Jack cheese
- 1 can (4-1/4 ounces) chopped ripe olives
- 4 fresh basil leaves, thinly sliced
- 3 garlic cloves, minced
- 1 teaspoon salt
- 1/2 teaspoon pepper
- 3/4 cup meatless spaghetti sauce
- 1/2 cup water
- 4 tablespoons grated Parmesan cheese, *divided*

1 Cut tops off peppers and remove seeds; set aside. In a large bowl, combine the rice, tomatoes, corn, onion and beans. Stir in the Monterey Jack cheese, olives, basil, garlic, salt and pepper. Spoon into peppers.

2 Combine spaghetti sauce and water; pour half into an oval 5-qt. slow cooker. Add the stuffed peppers. Top with remaining sauce. Sprinkle with 2 tablespoons Parmesan cheese.

3 Cover and cook on low for 3-1/2 to 4 hours or until peppers are tender and filling is heated through. Sprinkle with remaining Parmesan cheese.

YIELD: 6 SERVINGS.

barbecued beef short ribs

ERIN GLASS
WHITE HALL, MARYLAND

These slow-cooked ribs with a tangy sauce are a cinch to make. They're great for picnics and parties.

- 4 pounds bone-in beef short ribs, trimmed
- 2 tablespoons canola oil
- 1 large sweet onion, halved and sliced
- 1 bottle (12 ounces) chili sauce
- 3/4 cup plum preserves *or* preserves of your choice
- 2 tablespoons brown sugar
- 2 tablespoons red wine vinegar
- 2 tablespoons Worcestershire sauce
- 2 tablespoons Dijon mustard
- 1/4 teaspoon ground cloves

1 In a large skillet, brown ribs in oil in batches. Place onion in a 5-qt. slow cooker; add ribs. Cover and cook on low for 4-1/2 to 5 hours or until meat is tender.

2 In a small saucepan, combine the remaining ingredients. Cook and stir over medium heat for 4-6 minutes or until heated through.

3 Remove ribs from slow cooker. Skim fat from cooking juices. Return ribs to slow cooker; pour sauce over ribs. Cover and cook on high for 25-30 minutes or until sauce is thickened.

YIELD: 6 SERVINGS.

slow-cooked enchilada dinner

JUDY RAGSDALE
QUEEN CITY, TEXAS

This layered Southwestern meal just can't be beat. It gets its spicy flavor from green chilies, seasoned beans, chili powder and cumin.

- 1 pound lean ground beef (90% lean)
- 1 small onion, chopped
- 1 can (15 ounces) Ranch Style beans (pinto beans in seasoned tomato sauce)
- 1 can (10 ounces) diced tomatoes with mild green chilies, undrained
- 1/4 cup chopped green pepper
- 1 teaspoon chili powder
- 1/2 teaspoon *each* salt and ground cumin
- 1/4 teaspoon pepper
- 1 cup (4 ounces) shredded Monterey Jack cheese
- 1 cup (4 ounces) shredded cheddar cheese
- 6 flour tortillas (6 inches)

1 In a large skillet, cook beef and onion over medium heat until meat is no longer pink; drain. Stir in the beans, tomatoes, green pepper, chili powder, salt, cumin and pepper. In a small bowl, combine the cheeses; set aside.

2 Cut three 25-in. x 3-in. strips of foil; crisscross so they resemble spokes of a wheel. Place strips on the bottom and up the sides of a 5-qt. slow cooker. Coat strips with cooking spray. Place two tortillas in slow cooker, overlapping if necessary. Layer with a third of the beef mixture and cheese. Repeat layers twice.

3 Cover and cook on low for 2 to 2-1/2 hours or until heated through. Using foil strips as handles, remove enchilada dinner to a platter.

YIELD: 6 SERVINGS.

lemon chicken breasts

KATHY EVANS
LACEY, WASHINGTON

Dijon mustard, rosemary and lemon juice season chicken breasts wonderfully well in this fuss-free recipe. For an elegant and impressive finish, sprinkle on some toasted almonds and fresh parsley.

- 6 boneless skinless chicken breast halves (5 ounces *each*)
- 1 cup chicken broth, *divided*
- 1/4 cup lemon juice
- 3 tablespoons Dijon mustard
- 3 garlic cloves, minced
- 2 tablespoons butter, melted
- 1/4 teaspoon dried rosemary, crushed
- 3 tablespoons cornstarch

Hot cooked rice

- 1/2 cup slivered almonds, toasted
- 3 tablespoons minced fresh parsley

1 Place chicken in a 3-qt. slow cooker. In a small bowl, combine 3/4 cup broth, lemon juice, mustard, garlic, butter and rosemary; pour over chicken. Cover and cook on low for 4-5 hours or until a meat thermometer reads 170°. Remove chicken; keep warm.

2 Skim fat from cooking juices; transfer to a small saucepan. Bring liquid to a boil. Combine cornstarch and remaining chicken broth until smooth. Gradually stir into the pan. Bring to a boil; cook and stir for 2 minutes or until thickened. Serve chicken with rice and sauce. Sprinkle with almonds and parsley.

YIELD: 6 SERVINGS.

herbed turkey breasts

LAURIE MACE
LOS OSOS, CALIFORNIA

Tender, moist turkey breast is enhanced with an array of flavorful herbs in this comforting dish.

- 2 cans (14-1/2 ounces *each*) chicken broth
- 1 cup lemon juice
- 1/2 cup packed brown sugar
- 1/2 cup fresh sage
- 1/2 cup minced fresh thyme
- 1/2 cup *each* lime juice, cider vinegar and olive oil
- 2 envelopes onion soup mix
- 1/4 cup Dijon mustard
- 2 tablespoons minced fresh marjoram
- 3 teaspoons paprika
- 2 teaspoons garlic powder
- 2 teaspoons pepper
- 1 teaspoon salt
- 2 boneless turkey breasts (2 pounds *each*)

1 In a blender, process the first 15 ingredients in batches until blended. Pour 3-1/2 cups marinade into a large resealable plastic bag; add the turkey. Seal the bag and turn to coat; refrigerate for 8 hours or overnight. Cover and refrigerate the remaining marinade.

2 Drain and discard the marinade. Place the turkey in a 5-qt. slow cooker; add reserved marinade. Cover and cook on high for 3-1/2 to 4-1/2 hours or until a meat thermometer reads 170°.

YIELD: 14-16 SERVINGS.

freeze lemon juice

I like to keep fresh lemon juice on hand because it's such an easy way to add refreshing flavor to many recipes. After juicing the lemons, I freeze the juice in ice cube trays. Then I simply defrost them and use in poultry recipes, lemon desserts, iced or hot teas and many other dishes.

JUDY M., SOUTH BEND, INDIANA

mexican pork roast

CHUCK ALLEN
DANA POINT, CALIFORNIA

Friends who live in Mexico shared this recipe with me years ago. They cooked the roast in a clay pot in a slow oven, but I found it works well in a slow cooker. The leftovers make great burritos and tacos.

- 2 medium onions, sliced
- 2 medium carrots, sliced
- 2 jalapeno peppers, seeded and chopped
- 2 tablespoons olive oil
- 3 garlic cloves, minced
- 1/2 cup water
- 1/2 cup chicken broth
- 1 teaspoon ground coriander
- 1/2 teaspoon salt
- 1/2 teaspoon ground cumin
- 1/2 teaspoon dried oregano
- 1/4 teaspoon pepper
- 1 boneless pork shoulder butt roast (3 pounds)

1 In a large skillet, saute the onions, carrots and jalapenos in oil for 3 minutes. Add garlic; cook 1 minute longer. Transfer to a 5-qt. slow cooker; add water and broth.

2 In a small bowl, combine the coriander, salt, cumin, oregano and pepper; rub over roast. Cut roast in half; place in the slow cooker. Cover and cook on low for 8-9 hours or until meat is tender.

3 Transfer roast and vegetables to a serving platter; keep warm. Strain cooking juices and skim fat. Pour into a small saucepan. Bring to a boil; cook until liquid is reduced to about 1 cup. Serve with roast and vegetables.

YIELD: 8 SERVINGS.

EDITOR'S NOTE: When cutting hot peppers, disposable gloves are recommended. Avoid touching your face.

hearty short ribs

HELENA IVY
ST. LOUIS, MISSOURI

The whole family will love these ribs! The meat is so tender it simply falls off the bones, and the gravy is perfect with either mashed potatoes or rice.

- 1 large onion, sliced
- 4 pounds bone-in beef short ribs
- 1/2 pound sliced fresh mushrooms
- 1 can (10-3/4 ounces) condensed cream of mushroom soup, undiluted
- 1/2 cup water
- 1 envelope brown gravy mix
- 1 teaspoon minced garlic
- 1/2 teaspoon dried thyme
- 1 tablespoon cornstarch
- 2 tablespoons cold water
  Hot mashed potatoes

1 Place onion in a 5-qt. slow cooker; top with ribs. Combine the mushrooms, soup, 1/2 cup water, gravy mix, garlic and thyme; pour over ribs. Cover and cook on low for 6 to 6-1/2 hours or until meat is tender.

2 Remove meat to serving platter; keep warm. Skim fat from cooking juices; transfer to a small saucepan. Bring to a boil.

3 Combine cornstarch and cold water until smooth. Gradually stir into pan. Bring to a boil. Cook and stir for 2 minutes or until thickened. Serve with meat and mashed potatoes.

YIELD: 6 SERVINGS.

forgotten jambalaya

CINDI COSS
COPPELL, TEXAS

During chilly weather, I fix this jambalaya at least once a month. It's so easy—just chop the vegetables, dump everything in the slow cooker and forget it! Even my sons, who are picky about spicy foods, like this dish.

1 can (14-1/2 ounces) diced tomatoes, undrained
1 can (14-1/2 ounces) beef *or* chicken broth
1 can (6 ounces) tomato paste
2 medium green peppers, chopped
1 medium onion, chopped
3 celery ribs, chopped
5 garlic cloves, minced
3 teaspoons dried parsley flakes
2 teaspoons dried basil
1-1/2 teaspoons dried oregano
1-1/4 teaspoons salt
1/2 teaspoon cayenne pepper
1/2 teaspoon hot pepper sauce
1 pound boneless skinless chicken breasts, cut into 1-inch cubes
1 pound smoked sausage, halved and cut into 1/4-inch slices
1/2 pound uncooked medium shrimp, peeled and deveined
Hot cooked rice

1 In a 5-qt. slow cooker, combine the tomatoes, broth and tomato paste. Stir in the green peppers, onion, celery, garlic and seasonings. Stir in chicken and sausage.

2 Cover and cook on low for 4 hours or until chicken is tender. Stir in shrimp. Cover and cook 15-30 minutes longer or until shrimp turn pink. Serve with rice.

YIELD: 11 SERVINGS.

melt-in-your-mouth chuck roast

BETTE MCCUMBER
SCHENECTADY, NEW YORK

My husband and I like well-seasoned foods, so this recipe is terrific for us. You'll love how tasty and succulent this roast turns out.

- 1 large onion, sliced
- 1 medium green pepper, sliced
- 1 celery rib, chopped
- 1 boneless beef chuck roast (2 to 3 pounds)
- 1 can (14-1/2 ounces) Italian stewed tomatoes
- 1/2 cup *each* beef broth and ketchup
- 3 tablespoons brown sugar
- 2 tablespoons Worcestershire sauce
- 4-1/2 teaspoons prepared mustard
- 3 garlic cloves, minced
- 1 tablespoon soy sauce
- 2 teaspoons pepper
- 1/4 teaspoon crushed red pepper flakes
- 3 tablespoons cornstarch
- 1/4 cup cold water

1 Place the onion, green pepper and celery in a 5-qt. slow cooker; add the roast. In a large bowl, combine the tomatoes, broth, ketchup, brown sugar, Worcestershire sauce, mustard, garlic, soy sauce, pepper and pepper flakes; pour over meat. Cover and cook on low for 5-6 hours or until meat is tender.

2 Remove meat and vegetables; keep warm. Skim fat from cooking juices if necessary; transfer to a small saucepan. Combine cornstarch and cold water until smooth; stir into cooking juices. Bring to a boil; cook and stir for 2 minutes or until thickened. Serve with roast.

YIELD: 6 SERVINGS.

curried chicken with peaches

HEIDI MARTINEZ
COLORADO SPRINGS, COLORADO

I'm always looking for dinners I can prepare ahead of time. The chicken in this recipe cooks for hours in delicious seasonings, and peaches round out the amazing flavors.

- 1 broiler/fryer chicken (3 pounds), cut up
- 1/8 teaspoon salt
- 1/8 teaspoon pepper
- 1 can (29 ounces) sliced peaches
- 1/2 cup chicken broth
- 2 tablespoons butter, melted
- 1 tablespoon dried minced onion
- 2 teaspoons curry powder
- 2 garlic cloves, minced
- 1/4 teaspoon ground ginger
- 3 tablespoons cornstarch
- 3 tablespoons cold water
- 1/4 cup raisins

Toasted flaked coconut, optional

1 Place chicken in a 5-qt. slow cooker; sprinkle with salt and pepper. Drain peaches, reserving 1/2 cup juice; set peaches aside. In a small bowl, combine the broth, butter, onion, curry, garlic, ginger and reserved juice; pour over chicken. Cover and cook on low for 3-4 hours or until chicken juices run clear.

2 Remove chicken to a serving platter; keep warm. Mix cornstarch and water until smooth; stir into cooking juices. Add raisins. Cover and cook on high for 10-15 minutes or until gravy is thickened. Stir in peaches; heat through. Serve with chicken. Garnish with coconut if desired.

YIELD: 4 SERVINGS.

slow-cooked lamb chops

SANDRA MCKENZIE
BRAHAM, MINNESOTA

This is my favorite recipe for lamb chops. It's great for people who are trying lamb for the first time, since the meat turns out extra tender and yummy. I decided to wrap the chops in bacon because that's how I've always done venison. I think it really enhances the dish.

- 4 bacon strips
- 4 lamb shoulder blade chops, trimmed
- 2-1/4 cups thinly sliced peeled potatoes

- 1 cup thinly sliced carrots
- 1/2 teaspoon dried rosemary, crushed
- 1/4 teaspoon garlic powder
- 1/4 teaspoon *each* salt and pepper
- 1/4 cup chopped onion
- 2 garlic cloves, minced
- 1 can (10-3/4 ounces) condensed cream of mushroom soup, undiluted
- 1/3 cup 2% milk
- 1 jar (4-1/2 ounces) sliced mushrooms, drained

1 Wrap bacon around lamb chops; secure with toothpicks. Place in a 3-qt. slow cooker. Cover and cook on high for 1-1/2 hours.

2 Remove chops; discard toothpicks and bacon. Drain liquid from slow cooker. Add potatoes and carrots; top with lamb chops. Sprinkle with rosemary, garlic powder, salt, pepper, onion and garlic.

3 In a small bowl, combine soup and milk. Add mushrooms. Pour over the chops. Cover and cook on low for 4-6 hours or until meat and vegetables are tender.

YIELD: 4 SERVINGS.

don't lift the lid

Unless the recipe instructs you to stir in or add ingredients, refrain from lifting the lid while the slow cooker is cooking. Every time you lift the lid, steam is lost and you add 15 to 30 minutes of cooking time.

TASTE OF HOME TEST KITCHEN

hearty beans with beef

JAN BIEHL
LEESBURG, INDIANA

My husband raved about these beans after having them at a party, so I knew I had to get the recipe. It's perfect for get-togethers because you can mix it up a day early and toss it in the slow cooker a few hours before guests arrive. Ground beef makes it especially satisfying.

- 1 pound ground beef
- 1 medium onion, chopped
- 1 can (16 ounces) baked beans, undrained
- 1 can (15-1/2 ounces) butter beans, rinsed and drained
- 1/2 cup ketchup
- 1/3 cup packed brown sugar
- 1 tablespoon barbecue sauce
- 1/4 teaspoon Worcestershire sauce

1 In a large skillet, cook beef and onion over medium heat until meat is no longer pink; drain.

2 Transfer to a 5-qt. slow cooker. Stir in the remaining ingredients.

3 Cover and cook on high for 3-4 hours or until heated through.

YIELD: 8-10 SERVINGS.

slow-cooked italian chicken

DEANNA D'AURIA
BANNING, CALIFORNIA

With its nicely seasoned tomato sauce, this enticing chicken entree is especially good over pasta or rice. My father loved this dish.

- 4 boneless skinless chicken breast halves (4 ounces each)
- 1 can (14-1/2 ounces) chicken broth
- 1 can (14-1/2 ounces) stewed tomatoes, cut up
- 1 can (8 ounces) tomato sauce
- 1 medium green pepper, chopped
- 1 green onion, chopped
- 1 garlic clove, minced
- 3 teaspoons chili powder
- 1 teaspoon ground mustard
- 1/2 teaspoon garlic salt *or* garlic powder
- 1/2 teaspoon onion salt *or* onion powder
- 1/2 teaspoon pepper
- 1/3 cup all-purpose flour
- 1/2 cup cold water

Hot cooked pasta

1 Place chicken in a 3-qt. slow cooker. In a bowl, combine the broth, tomatoes, tomato sauce, green pepper, onion, garlic and seasonings; pour over chicken. Cover and cook on low for 4-5 hours or until meat is tender. Remove chicken and keep warm.

2 Pour cooking juices into a large saucepan; skim fat. Combine flour and cold water until smooth; stir into juices. Bring to a boil; cook and stir for 2 minutes or until thickened. Serve with chicken and pasta.

YIELD: 4 SERVINGS.

swiss steak supper

KATHLEEN ROMANIUK
CHOMEDEY, QUEBEC

This satisfying slow-cooked dinner is perfect for chasing away the chills on a cold winter night. To save a step, I keep peppered seasoned salt on hand to use instead of the seasoned salt and pepper.

1-1/2 pounds beef top round steak
1/2 teaspoon seasoned salt
1/4 teaspoon coarsely ground pepper
1 tablespoon canola oil
3 medium potatoes
1-1/2 cups fresh baby carrots
1 medium onion, sliced
1 can (14-1/2 ounces) Italian diced tomatoes
1 jar (12 ounces) home-style beef gravy
1 tablespoon minced fresh parsley

1 Cut steak into six serving-size pieces; flatten to 1/4-in. thickness. Rub with seasoned salt and pepper. In a large skillet, brown beef in oil on both sides; drain.

2 Cut each potato into eight wedges. In a 5-qt. slow cooker, layer the potatoes, carrots, beef and onion. Combine tomatoes and gravy; pour over the top.

3 Cover and cook on low for 5-1/2 to 6 hours or until meat and vegetables are tender. Sprinkle with parsley.

YIELD: 6 SERVINGS.

sweet 'n' sour sausage

BARBARA SCHUTZ
PANDORA, OHIO

Carrots, green pepper and pineapple lend gorgeous color to this sausage supper. Serve it with rice or chow mein noodles.

1 pound smoked kielbasa *or* Polish sausage, sliced
1 can (20 ounces) unsweetened pineapple chunks, undrained
1-1/2 cups fresh baby carrots, quartered lengthwise
1 large green pepper, cut into 1-inch pieces
1 medium onion, cut into chunks
1/3 cup packed brown sugar
1 tablespoon soy sauce
1/2 teaspoon chicken bouillon granules
1/4 teaspoon garlic powder
1/4 teaspoon ground ginger
2 tablespoons cornstarch
1/4 cup cold water
Hot cooked rice *or* chow mein noodles

1 In a 3-qt. slow cooker, combine the first 10 ingredients. Cover and cook on low for 4-5 hours.

2 Mix cornstarch and water until smooth; stir into sausage mixture. Cover and cook on high for 30 minutes or until thickened. Serve with rice.

YIELD: 6 SERVINGS.

slow-cooked pork roast

MARION LOWERY
MEDFORD, OREGON

This pork roast makes a wonderful summer meal, as the oven never needs heating. It's so flavorful, it's sure to become a favorite.

- 2 cans (8 ounces *each*) unsweetened crushed pineapple, undrained
- 1 cup barbecue sauce
- 2 tablespoons unsweetened apple juice
- 1 tablespoon minced fresh rosemary *or* 1 teaspoon dried rosemary, crushed
- 1 teaspoon minced garlic
- 2 teaspoons grated lemon peel
- 1 teaspoon Liquid Smoke, optional
- 1/2 teaspoon salt
- 1/4 teaspoon pepper
- 1 boneless pork loin roast (3 to 4 pounds)

1 In a large saucepan, combine the first nine ingredients. Bring to a boil. Reduce heat; simmer, uncovered, for 3 minutes.

2 Meanwhile, cut roast in half. In a nonstick skillet coated with cooking spray, brown pork roast.

3 Place roast in a 5-qt. slow cooker. Pour sauce over roast and turn to coat. Cook on low for 6-7 hours or until meat is tender. Let stand for 15 minutes before carving.

YIELD: 12 SERVINGS.

double-onion beef brisket

ELAINE SWEET
DALLAS, TEXAS

It's the slow cooking of this brisket that makes it so tender. It gets a wonderfully sweet-tangy flavor from chili sauce, cider vinegar and brown sugar.

- 1 fresh beef brisket (4 pounds)
- 1-1/2 teaspoons kosher salt *or* 1-1/4 teaspoons regular table salt
- 1-1/2 teaspoons coarsely ground pepper
- 2 tablespoons olive oil
- 3 medium onions, halved and sliced
- 3 celery ribs, chopped
- 1 cup chili sauce
- 1/4 cup packed brown sugar
- 1/4 cup cider vinegar
- 1 envelope onion soup mix

1 Cut brisket in half; sprinkle all sides with salt and pepper. In a large skillet, brown brisket in oil; remove and set aside. In the same skillet, cook and stir onions on low heat for 8-10 minutes or until caramelized.

2 Place half of the onions in a 5-qt. slow cooker; top with celery and brisket. Combine the chili sauce, brown sugar, vinegar and soup mix. Pour over brisket; top with remaining onions.

3 Cover and cook on low for 6-7 hours or until meat is tender. Let stand for 5 minutes before slicing. Skim fat from cooking juices and serve with meat.

YIELD: 10 SERVINGS.

EDITOR'S NOTE : This is a fresh beef brisket, not corned beef.

tender pork chops

BONNIE MARLOW
OTTOVILLE, OHIO

Not only is it easy to use my slow cooker, the results are fabulous. Meat cooked this way is always so tender and juicy. My pork chops, in a thick tomato sauce, always turn out perfectly.

- 6 boneless pork loin chops (1/2 inch thick and 6 ounces *each*)
- 1 tablespoon canola oil
- 1 medium green pepper, diced
- 1 can (6 ounces) tomato paste
- 1 jar (4-1/2 ounces) sliced mushrooms, drained
- 1/2 cup water
- 1 envelope spaghetti sauce mix
- 1/2 to 1 teaspoon hot pepper sauce

1 In a large skillet, brown pork chops in oil over medium heat for 3-4 minutes on each side; drain.

2 In a 5-qt. slow cooker, combine the remaining ingredients. Top with pork chops. Cover and cook on low for 5-1/2 to 6 hours or until meat is tender.

YIELD: 6 SERVINGS.

slow-cooked taco meat loaf

LACEY KIRSCH
THORNTON, COLORADO

This meat loaf is a hit with my family. My three sons eat two pieces each, which is incredible, considering that they are very picky eaters. A sweet and tangy sauce tops this Southwest-style meat loaf.

- 2 cups crushed tortilla chips
- 1 cup (4 ounces) shredded cheddar cheese
- 1 cup salsa
- 1/2 cup egg substitute
- 1/4 cup sliced ripe olives
- 1 envelope taco seasoning
- 2 pounds lean ground beef (90% lean)
- 1/2 cup ketchup
- 1/4 cup packed brown sugar
- 2 tablespoons Louisiana-style hot sauce

1 Cut four 20-in. x 3-in. strips of heavy-duty foil; crisscross so they resemble spokes of a wheel. Place strips on the bottom and up the sides of a 3-qt. slow cooker. Coat strips with cooking spray.

2 In a large bowl, combine the first six ingredients. Crumble beef over mixture and mix well. Shape into a round loaf. Place meat loaf in the center of the strips. Cover and cook on low for 3-4 hours or until no pink remains and a meat thermometer reads 160°.

3 Combine the ketchup, brown sugar and hot sauce; pour over meat loaf during the last hour of cooking. Let stand for 10 minutes. Using foil strips as handles, remove the meat loaf to a platter.

YIELD: 8 SERVINGS.

soups

« CHEESEBURGER PARADISE SOUP, P. 95

tortilla-vegetable chicken soup

JAN PERI-WYRICK
FORT WORTH, TEXAS

Surprisingly, this recipe is a snap. Don't worry about the long list of ingredients; most of them are already in your pantry.

- 3 flour tortillas (6 inches), cut into 1-inch strips
- 1/4 cup chicken drippings, optional
- 1 cup chopped celery
- 3/4 cup finely chopped carrot
- 1/2 cup chopped red onion
- 2 tablespoons olive oil
- 3 cans (14-1/2 ounces *each*) reduced-sodium chicken broth
- 1 can (15 ounces) black beans, rinsed and drained
- 1 can (14-1/2 ounces) beef broth
- 1 can (10 ounces) diced tomatoes with mild green chilies
- 2 cups cubed cooked chicken breast
- 2 cups frozen corn
- 2 teaspoons dried parsley flakes
- 1 teaspoon garlic powder
- 1 teaspoon dried basil
- 1 teaspoon ground cumin
- 2 teaspoons ground coriander

Shredded Monterey Jack cheese, optional

1 Place the tortilla strips on a baking sheet coated with cooking spray; bake at 350° for 8-10 minutes or until lightly browned. Set aside.

2 Meanwhile, skim fat from drippings. In a Dutch oven, saute the celery, carrot and onion in oil until tender. Stir in the chicken broth, black beans, beef broth, tomatoes, chicken, corn, seasonings and drippings if desired. Bring to a boil. Reduce the heat; simmer, uncovered, for 15 minutes.

3 Serve with cheese if desired and tortilla strips.

YIELD: 6 SERVINGS.

very veggie soup

JAIME SARGENT
FARMINGTON, NEW YORK

I created this soup in an effort to make my family's diet healthier. We have a bowl for lunch or with our dinner. It helps us get our daily servings of vegetables.

- 1 medium zucchini, chopped
- 1-1/3 cups chopped fresh mushrooms
- 1 small onion, chopped
- 1 teaspoon canola oil
- 4 garlic cloves, minced
- 1 carton (32 ounces) reduced-sodium chicken broth
- 2 cans (14-1/2 ounces *each*) diced tomatoes with basil, oregano and garlic, undrained
- 1 package (16 ounces) frozen chopped broccoli, thawed
- 2 medium carrots, shredded
- 1 cup meatless spaghetti sauce
- 1 teaspoon Italian seasoning
- 1 teaspoon adobo seasoning
- 1 package (10 ounces) frozen chopped spinach, thawed and squeezed dry

Parmesan cheese

1 In a Dutch oven, saute the zucchini, mushrooms and onion in oil until tender. Add garlic; cook 1 minute longer. Add the broth, tomatoes, broccoli, carrots, spaghetti sauce and the seasonings.

2 Bring to a boil. Reduce heat; cover and simmer 10-15 minutes or until vegetables are tender. Stir in spinach; heat through. Garnish each serving with cheese.

YIELD: 6 SERVINGS (2 QUARTS).

hearty italian soup

ROBIN SABROWSKY
PLYMOUTH, WISCONSIN

Macaroni and Italian sausage make this tomato-veggie soup thick and delicious. It offers a nice change of pace from my chili recipe.

- 1 Italian sausage link, cut into 1/2-inch pieces
- 1 small onion, chopped
- 1/2 medium green pepper, chopped
- 1 can (14-1/2 ounces) Italian diced tomatoes, undrained
- 1-1/2 cups water
- 1 can (8 ounces) tomato sauce
- 1 teaspoon sugar
- 1 teaspoon chicken bouillon granules
- 1/4 teaspoon garlic powder
- 1/3 cup uncooked elbow macaroni
- 2 tablespoons shredded part-skim mozzarella cheese

1 In a large saucepan, cook the sausage, onion and green pepper until sausage is browned; drain. Stir in the tomatoes, water, tomato sauce, sugar, bouillon and garlic powder. Bring to a boil. Reduce heat; cover and simmer for 15 minutes, stirring occasionally.

2 Stir in macaroni. Cover and simmer 10-15 minutes longer or until macaroni is tender. Sprinkle with cheese.

YIELD: 4 CUPS.

meatball minestrone

LINDA DE BEAUDRAP
CALGARY, ALBERTA

As the busy parents of two boys, we are always looking for quick meals. You simply warm the meatballs for this satisfying soup, so it's table-ready in moments.

- 6 cups water
- 1 can (16 ounces) kidney beans, rinsed and drained
- 1 package (16 ounces) frozen mixed vegetables
- 2 tablespoons beef bouillon granules
- 1 tablespoon dried minced onion
- 1 bay leaf
- 1 teaspoon salt
- 1 teaspoon dried basil
- 1/2 teaspoon pepper
- 4 ounces spaghetti, broken into 2-inch pieces
- 1 package (12 ounces) frozen fully cooked homestyle meatballs
- 1 can (14-1/2 ounces) stewed tomatoes

1 In a Dutch oven, bring the first nine ingredients to a boil.

2 Add spaghetti. Reduce heat; simmer 10 minutes or until spaghetti is tender. Add meatballs and tomatoes; heat through. Discard the bay leaf.

YIELD: 10-12 SERVINGS.

"apres-ski" soup

NANCY HAMLIN
LITTLETON, COLORADO

Apres-ski, French for "after skiing," refers to the social time directly after getting off the slopes, and this microwave soup is perfect for the occasion. Full of healthy veggies, this one will warm you up!

- 1 tablespoon butter
- 1-1/4 cups cubed acorn squash
- 1 carrot, thinly sliced
- 1 medium leek (white portion only), thinly sliced
- 3 cans (14-1/2 ounces *each*) reduced-sodium chicken broth
- 1 small zucchini, halved and sliced
- 1/2 cup uncooked elbow macaroni
- 1 bay leaf
- 1/2 teaspoon dried basil
- 1/4 teaspoon dried thyme
- 1/8 teaspoon *each* salt and pepper

1 Place butter in a 3-qt. microwave-safe bowl; microwave on high for 20-30 seconds or until melted. Add the squash, carrot and leek; stir to coat. Cover and cook on high for 6 minutes.

2 Stir in the remaining ingredients; cover and cook on high for 12-14 minutes or until vegetables and macaroni are tender, stirring twice. Discard bay leaf.

YIELD: 6 SERVINGS.

EDITOR'S NOTE: This recipe was tested in a 1,100-watt microwave.

chipotle butternut squash soup

ROXANNE CHAN
ALBANY, CALIFORNIA

Using herbs and vegetables from the garden along with convenient pantry items makes this specialty fast to fix. Your family will devour it.

- 2 cups diced peeled butternut squash
- 1 small carrot, finely chopped
- 1 green onion, sliced
- 1/2 teaspoon ground cumin
- 1 tablespoon olive oil
- 2 garlic cloves, minced
- 2 cups vegetable broth, *divided*
- 1 can (14-1/2 ounces) diced tomatoes, undrained
- 1 package (3 ounces) cream cheese, cubed
- 1/4 cup minced fresh basil
- 1 chipotle pepper in adobo sauce, chopped
- 1 can (15 ounces) black beans, rinsed and drained
- 1 can (11 ounces) Mexicorn, drained
- 2 cups fresh baby spinach

1 In a large saucepan, saute the squash, carrot, onion and cumin in oil for 10 minutes. Add garlic; cook 1 minute longer. Add 1-1/2 cups broth; bring to a boil. Reduce heat. Cover and simmer for 10-12 minutes or until vegetables are tender; cool slightly.

2 Transfer mixture to a blender; add the tomatoes, cream cheese, basil, chipotle pepper and remaining broth. Cover and process for 1-2 minutes or until smooth.

3 Return to the saucepan; stir in the beans, corn and spinach. Cook and stir until spinach is wilted and soup is heated through.

YIELD: 5 SERVINGS.

EDITOR'S NOTE: If garnish is desired, sprinkle butternut squash seeds with 1/8 teaspoon salt. Place on a baking sheet. Bake at 350° for 10-13 minutes or until golden brown.

fresh tomato soup

DONALD BONG
HAGER CITY, WISCONSIN

My gang doesn't care for traditional tomato soup, but they love this rich, fresh-tasting version. It has an unexpected chicken-broth base and appealing chunks of tomatoes. It's an excellent first course and a great light lunch with a salad and garlic bread.

- 2 cups sliced carrots
- 1 cup chopped celery
- 1 small onion, finely chopped
- 1/2 cup chopped green pepper
- 1/4 cup butter
- 4-1/2 cups chicken broth, *divided*
- 4 medium tomatoes, peeled and chopped (4 cups)
- 4 teaspoons sugar
- 1/2 teaspoon curry powder
- 1/2 teaspoon salt, optional
- 1/4 teaspoon pepper
- 1/4 cup all-purpose flour

1 In a Dutch oven, saute carrots, celery, onion and green pepper in butter until tender. Add 4 cups broth, tomatoes, sugar, curry powder, salt if desired and pepper; bring to a boil. Reduce heat; simmer for 20 minutes.

2 In a small bowl, combine the flour and remaining broth until smooth. Gradually add to soup. Bring to a boil; cook and stir for 2 minutes.

YIELD: 9 SERVINGS (ABOUT 2 QUARTS).

italian vegetable soup

PHYLLIS SCHMALZ
KANSAS CITY, KANSAS

With macaroni, kidney beans, tomatoes, zucchini and lots of other veggies, this flavorful soup makes a hearty dinner.

- 2 medium carrots, diced
- 1 small onion, chopped
- 1 tablespoon olive oil
- 2 garlic cloves, minced
- 2 cans (14-1/2 ounces *each*) beef broth
- 1 can (14-1/2 ounces) diced tomatoes, undrained
- 2 cups water
- 1 small zucchini, diced
- 1 teaspoon dried basil
- 1 teaspoon salt
- 1/2 teaspoon dried oregano
- 1/4 teaspoon pepper
- 2 to 3 drops hot pepper sauce
- 1 can (16 ounces) kidney beans, rinsed and drained
- 1 cup chopped fresh spinach
- 3/4 cup uncooked elbow macaroni
- 2 tablespoons minced fresh parsley
- 1/2 cup shredded Parmesan cheese

1 In a Dutch oven, saute carrots and onion in oil until tender. Add garlic; cook 1 minute longer. Stir in the broth, tomatoes, water, zucchini, basil, salt, oregano, pepper and hot pepper sauce. Bring to a boil. Reduce heat; cover and simmer for 15 minutes.

2 Stir in the kidney beans, spinach, macaroni and parsley. Cover and cook 15 minutes longer or until macaroni is tender. Garnish with cheese.

YIELD: 6-8 SERVINGS.

chunky chicken soup

TASTE OF HOME TEST KITCHEN

Featuring beans, chicken and veggies, this quick soup is a filling family-pleaser, and it tastes like it's been cooking all day!

- 3/4 pound boneless skinless chicken breasts, cut into 1/2-inch cubes
- 1/2 cup chopped onion
- 2 teaspoons olive oil
- 1-1/2 teaspoons minced garlic
- 2 tablespoons all-purpose flour
- 2 cans (14-1/2 ounces *each*) vegetable broth
- 2 cans (15-1/2 ounces *each*) great northern beans, rinsed and drained
- 1-1/2 cups frozen mixed vegetables, thawed
- 1 cup frozen chopped broccoli, thawed
- 1 can (4 ounces) chopped green chilies
- 3/4 teaspoon Italian seasoning
- 1/2 teaspoon ground cumin
- 1/4 teaspoon pepper
- 1/2 cup shredded part-skim mozzarella cheese

1 In a Dutch oven, saute chicken and onion in oil until chicken is no longer pink. Add garlic; cook 1 minute longer. Stir in flour until blended; gradually add broth. Bring to a boil; cook and stir for 2 minutes or until thickened.

2 Reduce heat; stir in the beans, vegetables and seasonings. Cook, stirring occasionally, for 8-10 minutes or until vegetables are tender. Garnish with cheese.

YIELD: 7 CUPS.

hearty minestrone

KATIE KOZIOLEK
HARTLAND, MINNESOTA

This is my all-time favorite soup! I love to make big batches and freeze some for later. It's so substantial it reminds me of spaghetti and sauce in soup form!

- 1 pound ground pork
- 1/2 cup chopped celery
- 1/2 cup chopped onion
- 1/2 teaspoon minced garlic
- 1 can (28 ounces) crushed tomatoes
- 1 can (16 ounces) kidney beans, rinsed and drained
- 1 can (15 ounces) garbanzo beans *or* chickpeas, rinsed and drained
- 2 cups tomato juice
- 1 can (15 ounces) tomato sauce
- 1 can (14-1/2 ounces) beef broth
- 3 medium carrots, chopped
- 1 medium zucchini, halved lengthwise and thinly sliced
- 1 tablespoon Italian seasoning
- 1 to 1-1/2 teaspoons salt
- 1/2 teaspoon sugar, optional
- 1/8 teaspoon pepper

ADDITIONAL INGREDIENTS (for each batch):

- 1/2 cup water
- 1 cup uncooked ziti *or* small tube pasta

1 In a Dutch oven, cook the pork, celery and onion over medium heat until meat is no longer pink. Add garlic; cook 1 minute longer. Drain.

2 Stir in tomatoes, beans, tomato juice, tomato sauce, broth, carrots, zucchini, Italian seasoning, salt, sugar if desired and pepper. Bring to a boil. Reduce heat; cover and simmer for 30-35 minutes or until carrots are tender.

3 Transfer 6 cups of soup to a freezer container; freeze for up to 3 months. Add water and pasta to remaining soup; bring to a boil. Cover and cook until pasta is tender.

4 **To use frozen soup:** Thaw in the refrigerator; transfer to a large saucepan. Stir in water. Bring to a boil; reduce heat. Add pasta; cover and cook until tender.

YIELD: 2 BATCHES (6 SERVINGS EACH).

curried apple soup

XAVIER PENNELL
MAULDIN, SOUTH CAROLINA

Harvest-fresh soup is a perfect salute to the riches of Indian summer. Here, sweet apples, spicy curry and tangy lemon strike a delicious balance.

- 1 medium onion, chopped
- 2 tablespoons butter
- 1 teaspoon curry powder
- 1/4 teaspoon ground cinnamon
- 1/8 teaspoon salt
- Dash cayenne pepper
- Dash ground cloves
- 3 medium McIntosh apples, peeled and sliced
- 3 cups chicken broth
- 1-1/2 teaspoons lemon juice
- Crackers and additional ground cinnamon, optional

1 In a small saucepan, saute onion in butter until tender. Add the curry, cinnamon, salt, cayenne and cloves; cook and stir for 1 minute. Add apples and broth; bring to a boil. Reduce heat; cover and simmer for 5-7 minutes or until apples are tender.

2 In a blender, puree soup until smooth. Return to the pan. Stir in lemon juice and heat through. Garnish with crackers and additional cinnamon if desired.

YIELD: 4 SERVINGS.

4-1/2 cups chicken broth

1 package (16 ounces) frozen sugar snap stir-fry vegetable blend, thawed

1 can (15-1/2 ounces) great northern beans, rinsed and drained

1 teaspoon ground mustard

1 cup biscuit/baking mix

2/3 cup cornmeal

1/4 teaspoon dried oregano

1/4 teaspoon dried basil

2/3 cup 2% milk

1/2 cup uncooked orzo pasta

1 In a Dutch oven, saute the onion in oil until tender. Stir in the broth, vegetable blend, beans and mustard. Bring to a boil. Reduce the heat; simmer for 6-8 minutes or until heated through.

2 For dumplings, in a small bowl, combine the baking mix, cornmeal, oregano and basil. Stir in milk just until moistened; set aside.

3 Stir orzo into soup. Drop the dumpling batter by tablespoonfuls into simmering soup. Cover and simmer for 20 minutes or until a toothpick inserted in a dumpling comes out clean (do not lift the cover while simmering).

YIELD: 6 SERVINGS (2 QUARTS).

southwestern soup

JEAN ECOS
HARTLAND, WISCONSIN

Herbs and spices add zest to this tomato-basil-based soup. With corn, salsa and beans, this recipe is guaranteed to spice up a cool night.

3 cups water

4 cans (8 ounces *each*) tomato sauce

2 cans (16 ounces *each*) kidney beans, rinsed and drained

2 cans (14-1/2 ounces *each*) chicken broth

2 cups frozen corn

2 cups salsa

2 teaspoons dried minced onion

1 to 2 teaspoons dried oregano

1 to 2 teaspoons dried basil

2 cups (8 ounces) shredded cheddar cheese

Tortilla chips, optional

1 In a Dutch oven, combine the first nine ingredients. Bring to a boil. Reduce heat; simmer, uncovered, for 10-15 minutes or until heated through.

2 Sprinkle individual servings with cheese. Serve with tortilla chips if desired.

YIELD: 12 SERVINGS (4 QUARTS).

vegetable dumpling soup

GRACIELA SANDVIGEN
ROCHESTER, NEW YORK

As a busy working mother, I love this recipe. I can use common pantry items to put a hearty, healthful dinner on the table for my family or guests to enjoy.

1 medium onion, chopped

1 tablespoon canola oil

vegetarian black bean soup

HEATHER BALDRY
KNOXVILLE, TENNESSEE

Here's a chunky soup that is chock-full of hearty ingredients such as potatoes and black beans. The tasty vegetable broth is a nice change from chicken or beef.

- 1 cup chopped onion
- 2 garlic cloves, minced
- 1 can (14-1/2 ounces) vegetable broth, *divided*
- 2 cans (15 ounces *each*) black beans, rinsed and drained
- 1 cup diced peeled potato
- 1/2 teaspoon dried thyme
- 1/2 teaspoon ground cumin
- 1 can (14-1/2 ounces) diced tomatoes, undrained
- 1/4 to 1/2 teaspoon hot pepper sauce
- 2 green onions, sliced

1 In a large saucepan, bring the onion, garlic and 1/4 cup broth to a boil. Reduce heat; cover and simmer for 6-8 minutes or until onion is tender. Stir in the beans, potato, thyme, cumin and remaining broth; return to a boil. Reduce heat; cover and simmer for 20-25 minutes or until potatoes are tender.

2 Stir in tomatoes and hot pepper sauce; heat through. Sprinkle with green onions.

YIELD: 6 SERVINGS.

wild rice chicken soup

TASTE OF HOME TEST KITCHEN

This substantial soup is brimming with tender chicken thigh meat and veggies, pleasantly seasoned with savory and garlic.

- 1/4 cup *each* chopped carrot, celery, green pepper and onion
- 1/4 cup chopped peeled parsnip
- 2 teaspoons canola oil
- 2 cans (14-1/2 ounces *each*) chicken broth
- 3/4 pound bone-in chicken thighs, skin removed
- 1/2 teaspoon dried savory
- 1 garlic clove, minced
- 1/8 teaspoon salt
- 1/8 teaspoon pepper
- 1 cup cooked long grain and wild rice

1 In a large saucepan, saute the carrot, celery, green pepper, onion and parsnip in oil for 3 minutes or until crisp-tender. Add the broth, chicken, savory, garlic, salt and pepper. Bring to a boil. Reduce heat; cover and simmer for 15 minutes or until chicken is no longer pink.

2 Remove chicken from broth. When cool enough to handle, remove meat from bones and cut into bite-size pieces. Discard bones. Add chicken and rice to soup; heat through.

YIELD: 5 SERVINGS.

carrots add spark to wild rice

Next time you're making wild rice, add a cup or two of shredded carrots shortly before you're done cooking. You'll enjoy the extra crunch!

CONNIE D., KNOXVILLE, TENNESSEE

southwestern tomato soup

SHERRI JACKSON
CHILLICOTHE, OHIO

When the season's ripest tomatoes are available and the weather starts to cool, I turn to this recipe. It will warm you from the inside out.

- 10 plum tomatoes, halved lengthwise
- 1 to 2 Anaheim peppers, halved and seeded
- 1/2 cup chopped onion
- 2 garlic cloves, minced
- 1 tablespoon olive oil
- 2 cans (14-1/2 ounces *each*) chicken broth
- 1 tablespoon minced fresh cilantro
- 2 teaspoons ground cumin
- 1/2 teaspoon sugar
- 1/2 teaspoon salt
- 1/4 teaspoon pepper
- Oil for frying
- 8 corn tortillas (6 inches), cut into 1/4-inch strips
- Sour cream, optional

1 Place tomatoes cut side down on a broiler pan; broil 3-4 in. from the heat for 15-20 minutes. Peel and discard skins. Repeat with peppers, broiling for 5-10 minutes.

2 In a small skillet, saute onion and garlic in oil until tender. Transfer to a blender; add tomatoes and peppers. Cover and process until smooth.

3 Press mixture through a strainer with a spoon; discard seeds. Transfer mixture to a large saucepan. Stir in the chicken broth, cilantro, cumin, sugar, salt and pepper. Cover and cook on low for 15 minutes or until heated through.

4 Meanwhile, heat 1/2 in. of oil in a skillet to 375°. Fry tortilla strips, in batches, for 3-5 minutes or until golden brown; drain on paper towels. Garnish bowls of soup with tortilla strips. Serve with sour cream if desired.

YIELD: 6 SERVINGS.

EDITOR'S NOTE: We recommend wearing disposable gloves when cutting hot peppers. Avoid touching your face.

tortellini soup

MARSHA FARLEY
BANGOR, MAINE

My soup is delicious, pretty and unbelievably fast to make. For a creamy variation, I sometimes substitute cream of mushroom soup for the French onion soup. If there are any leftovers, they taste even better the next day.

- 1 pound ground beef
- 3-1/2 cups water
- 1 can (28 ounces) diced tomatoes, undrained
- 1 can (10-1/2 ounces) condensed French onion soup, undiluted
- 1 package (9 ounces) frozen cut green beans
- 1 package (9 ounces) refrigerated cheese tortellini
- 1 medium zucchini, chopped
- 1 teaspoon dried basil

1 In a large saucepan, cook beef over medium heat until no longer pink; drain.

2 Add the remaining ingredients; bring to a boil. Cook, uncovered, for 7-9 minutes or until tortellini is tender.

YIELD: 6-8 SERVINGS.

EDITOR'S NOTE: Alongside Tortellini Soup, serve refrigerated crescent rolls. Before baking, sprinkle the rolls with Parmesan cheese.

hot italian sausage soup

DAN BUTE
OTTAWA, ILLINOIS

Loaded with zesty sausage and an array of veggies, this soup will hit the spot! A hint of brown sugar balances the heat with a little sweetness, making it a real crowd-pleaser. I'm part owner of a small tavern, and on Saturdays, we provide soups and deli sandwiches free of charge. Our patrons love this one.

  1 pound bulk hot Italian sausage
  1 can (14-1/2 ounces) Italian stewed tomatoes
  1 can (8 ounces) tomato sauce
  1 cup frozen Italian vegetables
  3/4 cup julienned green, sweet red *and/or* yellow pepper
  1/4 cup chopped onion
  1/4 cup white wine *or* chicken broth
  1 teaspoon brown sugar
  1 teaspoon minced fresh parsley
  1/2 teaspoon Italian seasoning
  1/8 teaspoon salt
  1/8 teaspoon pepper

1 In a large skillet, cook sausage over medium heat until no longer pink.

2 Meanwhile, in a large saucepan, combine the remaining ingredients. Bring to a boil. Reduce heat; cover and simmer for 10 minutes or until vegetables are tender.

3 Drain sausage; add to soup and heat through.

YIELD: 4 SERVINGS.

kielbasa cabbage soup

PATRICIA BOSSEE
DARIEN CENTER, NEW YORK

Cabbage is plentiful in upstate New York. During winter, I like to keep satisfying soups like this one simmering on the stovetop all day.

  1 small head cabbage, coarsely chopped
  1 medium onion, chopped
  4 to 6 garlic cloves, minced
  2 tablespoons olive oil
  4 cups water
  3 tablespoons cider vinegar
  1 to 2 tablespoons brown sugar
  1 pound smoked kielbasa *or* Polish sausage, halved, cut into 1/2-inch pieces
  4 medium potatoes, peeled and cubed
  3 large carrots, chopped
  1 teaspoon caraway seeds
  1/2 teaspoon pepper

1 In a Dutch oven or soup kettle, saute the cabbage, onion and garlic in oil for 5 minutes or until tender. Combine the water, vinegar and brown sugar; add to cabbage mixture.

2 Stir in remaining ingredients. Bring to a boil. Reduce heat; cover and simmer for 60-70 minutes or until vegetables are tender.

YIELD: 8-10 SERVINGS.

florentine chicken soup

CINDIE HENF
SEBASTIAN, FLORIDA

My husband loves Alfredo sauce, so I'm always looking for new variations. This easy-to-make soup is wonderful with crusty Italian bread and a tomato-mozzarella-basil salad. Best of all, it's the perfect amount for two of us.

- 1 cup uncooked penne pasta
- 1 package (6 ounces) ready-to-use chicken breast cuts
- 4 cups chopped fresh spinach
- 1 jar (7 ounces) roasted sweet red peppers, drained and sliced
- 3 fresh rosemary sprigs, chopped
- 1/2 teaspoon garlic powder
- 1/4 teaspoon pepper
- 1 tablespoon butter
- 1-1/2 cups reduced-sodium chicken broth
- 3/4 cup Alfredo sauce
- 3 tablespoons prepared pesto
- 2 tablespoons pine nuts, toasted
- 1 tablespoon shredded Parmesan cheese

1 Cook pasta according to package directions. Meanwhile, in a large saucepan, saute the chicken, spinach, red peppers, rosemary, garlic powder and pepper in butter until spinach is wilted. Stir in the broth, Alfredo sauce and pesto; cook for 4-5 minutes or until heated through.

2 Drain pasta and add to the soup. Sprinkle with pine nuts and cheese.

YIELD: 5 CUPS.

swiss chard bean soup

TASTE OF HOME TEST KITCHEN

For a hearty dish that combines nutritious Swiss chard with other garden favorites, consider the following recipe. Its light broth is surprisingly rich in flavor, and the grated Parmesan packs an additional punch.

- 1 medium carrot, coarsely chopped
- 1 small zucchini, coarsely chopped
- 1 small yellow summer squash, coarsely chopped
- 1 small red onion, chopped
- 2 tablespoons olive oil
- 2 garlic cloves, minced
- 3 cans (14-1/2 ounces *each*) reduced-sodium chicken broth
- 4 cups chopped Swiss chard
- 1 can (15-1/2 ounces) great northern beans, rinsed and drained
- 1 can (14-1/2 ounces) diced tomatoes, undrained
- 1 teaspoon dried thyme
- 1/2 teaspoon salt
- 1/2 teaspoon dried oregano
- 1/4 teaspoon pepper
- 1/4 cup grated Parmesan cheese

1 In a Dutch oven, saute the carrot, zucchini, yellow squash and onion in oil until tender. Add garlic; saute 1 minute longer. Add the broth, Swiss chard, beans, tomatoes, thyme, salt, oregano and pepper.

2 Bring to a boil. Reduce heat; simmer, uncovered, for 15 minutes or until chard is tender. Just before serving, sprinkle with cheese.

YIELD: 10 SERVINGS (2-1/2 QUARTS).

matzo ball soup

TASTE OF HOME TEST KITCHEN

You can make the soup a day ahead and reheat it just before serving.

- 10 cups water
- 12 garlic cloves, peeled
- 3 medium carrots, cut into chunks
- 3 small turnips, peeled and cut into chunks
- 2 medium onions, cut into wedges
- 2 medium parsnips, peeled and cut into chunks
- 1 medium leek (white portion only), sliced
- 1/4 cup minced fresh parsley
- 2 tablespoons snipped fresh dill
- 1 teaspoon salt
- 1 teaspoon pepper
- 3/4 teaspoon ground turmeric

MATZO BALLS:
- 3 eggs, *separated*
- 3 tablespoons water *or* chicken broth
- 3 tablespoons rendered chicken fat
- 1-1/2 teaspoons salt, *divided*
- 3/4 cup matzo meal
- 8 cups water

1 For broth, in a large soup kettle, combine the first 12 ingredients. Bring to a boil. Reduce heat; cover and simmer for 2 hours.

2 Meanwhile, in a large bowl, beat the egg yolks on high speed for 2 minutes or until thick and lemon-colored. Add the water, chicken fat and 1/2 teaspoon salt. In another bowl, beat egg whites on high until stiff peaks form; fold into yolk mixture. Fold in matzo meal. Cover and refrigerate for at least 1 hour or until thickened.

3 In another large soup kettle, bring water to a boil; add remaining salt. Drop eight rounded tablespoonfuls of matzo ball dough into boiling water. Reduce heat; cover and simmer for 20-25 minutes or until a toothpick inserted into a matzo ball comes out clean (do not lift cover while simmering).

4 Strain broth, discarding vegetables and seasonings. Carefully remove matzo balls from water with a slotted spoon; place one matzo ball in each soup bowl. Add broth.

YIELD: 8 SERVINGS.

macaroni vegetable soup

EDNA HOFFMAN
HEBRON, INDIANA

My colorful veggie soup gets its zing from a hint of cayenne pepper. A nice change of pace from heavy cream soups, the tasty, nutritious combination can be served as a side dish or light meal.

- 1 medium zucchini, julienned
- 1/2 cup finely chopped onion
- 1 medium carrot, halved and thinly sliced
- 1 tablespoon butter
- 2 cans (14-1/2 ounces *each*) chicken broth
- 1 cup tomato *or* vegetable juice
- 1/2 cup uncooked elbow macaroni
- 1/8 to 1/4 teaspoon cayenne pepper
- 1 can (15 ounces) white kidney *or* cannellini beans, rinsed and drained
- 1/2 cup frozen corn

1 In a large saucepan, saute the zucchini, onion and carrot in butter until tender. Add broth and tomato juice. Bring to a boil; stir in macaroni and cayenne. Cook for 10 minutes or until macaroni is tender. Stir in beans and corn; heat through.

YIELD: 8 SERVINGS (2 QUARTS).

danish turkey dumpling soup

KAREN SUE GARBACK-PRISTERA
ALBANY, NEW YORK

This recipe was handed down from my grandmother, who was a Danish caterer. My 100 percent Italian husband has come to expect it on a chilly evening, as it warms not only the body but the heart as well.

- 1 leftover turkey carcass (from a 12- to 14-pound turkey)
- 9 cups water
- 3 teaspoons chicken bouillon granules
- 1 bay leaf
- 1 can (14-1/2 ounces) stewed tomatoes, cut up
- 1 medium turnip, peeled and diced
- 2 celery ribs, chopped
- 1 medium onion, chopped
- 1 medium carrot, chopped
- 1/4 cup minced fresh parsley
- 1 teaspoon salt

DUMPLINGS

- 1/2 cup water
- 1/4 cup butter, cubed
- 1/2 cup all-purpose flour
- 1 teaspoon baking powder
- 1/8 teaspoon salt
- 2 eggs
- 1 tablespoon minced fresh parsley

1 Place carcass, water, bouillon and bay leaf in a stockpot. Bring to a boil. Reduce heat; cover and simmer for 1-1/2 hours.

2 Remove carcass. Strain broth and skim fat; discard bay leaf. Return broth to pan. Add the tomatoes, vegetables, parsley and salt. Remove turkey from bones and cut into bite-size pieces; add to soup. Discard bones. Bring to a boil. Reduce heat; cover and simmer for 25-30 minutes or until vegetables are crisp-tender.

3 For dumplings, in a large saucepan, bring water and butter to a boil. Combine the flour, baking powder and salt; add all at once to pan and stir until a smooth ball forms. Remove from heat; let stand for 5 minutes. Add eggs, one at a time, beating well after each addition. Continue beating until mixture is smooth and shiny. Stir in parsley.

1 Drop batter in 12 mounds into simmering soup. Cover and simmer for 20 minutes or until a toothpick inserted in a dumpling comes out clean (do not lift cover while simmering).

YIELD: 6 SERVINGS (ABOUT 2 QUARTS).

creamy bacon mushroom soup

NATHAN MERCER
INMAN, SOUTH CAROLINA

I've always enjoyed cooking, and I recently created this rich soup. It's a hit any time of year. You can also garnish it with chopped green onion tops or shredded Swiss cheese. For a smoother consistency, try pouring the soup through a strainer.

- 10 bacon strips, diced
- 1 pound sliced fresh mushrooms
- 1 medium onion, chopped
- 3 garlic cloves, minced
- 1 quart heavy whipping cream
- 1 can (14-1/2 ounces) chicken broth
- 1-1/4 cups shredded Swiss cheese
- 3 tablespoons cornstarch
- 1/2 teaspoon salt
- 1/2 teaspoon pepper
- 3 tablespoons water

1 In a large saucepan, cook bacon over medium heat until crisp. Using a slotted spoon, remove to paper towels; drain, reserving 2 tablespoons drippings. In the drippings, saute the mushrooms, onion and garlic. Stir in cream and broth. Gradually stir in cheese until melted.

2 In a small bowl, combine the cornstarch, salt, pepper and water until smooth. Stir into soup. Bring to a boil; cook and stir for 2 minutes or until thickened. Garnish with bacon.

YIELD: 8 SERVINGS (2 QUARTS).

buying & storing bacon

Always check the date stamp on vacuum-sealed bacon to make sure it's fresh. The date reflects the last day it should be sold. Once the package is opened, bacon should be used within a week. For long-term storage, freeze bacon for up to 1 month.

TASTE OF HOME TEST KITCHEN

creamy carrot soup

CAROLE MARTIN
COFFEEVILLE, MISSISSIPPI

I first sampled this colorful carrot soup at a local Victorian tearoom, and I wouldn't leave until I had the recipe in hand. The chef was kind enough to share it with me so I could enjoy it at home.

- 3/4 cup chopped onion
- 3 tablespoons butter, *divided*
- 3 cups chopped carrots
- 3 cups chicken broth
- 2 tablespoons uncooked long grain rice
- 1/2 cup heavy whipping cream
- 1 to 2 tablespoons tomato paste
- 1/2 teaspoon salt
- 1/4 teaspoon white pepper

1 In a large saucepan, saute the onion in 2 tablespoons butter. Add the carrots, broth and rice. Bring to a boil. Reduce heat; cover and simmer for 25 minutes or until carrots and rice are tender. Cool slightly.

2 Transfer to a blender; cover and process until smooth. Return to the pan. Add the cream, tomato paste, salt, pepper and remaining butter; heat through.

YIELD: 4-5 SERVINGS.

herbed potato soup

JO CROUCH
EAST ALTON, ILLINOIS

This creamy potato soup is almost as easy to make as opening a can of soup—and it tastes so much better. The rosemary and thyme add just the right amount of seasoning.

- 3 medium potatoes, peeled and diced
- 2 cups water

- 1 large onion, chopped
- 1/4 cup butter, cubed
- 1/4 cup all-purpose flour
- 1 teaspoon salt
- 1/2 teaspoon dried thyme
- 1/4 teaspoon dried rosemary, crushed
- 1/4 teaspoon pepper
- 1-1/2 cups milk

1 Place potatoes in a large saucepan and cover with water. Bring to a boil. Reduce heat; cover and simmer for 15-20 minutes or until tender.

2 Meanwhile, in another large saucepan, saute onion in butter until tender. Stir in the flour, salt, thyme, rosemary and pepper until blended. Gradually add milk. Bring to a boil; cook and stir for 2 minutes or until thickened. Add potatoes with cooking liquid; heat through.

YIELD: 5 SERVINGS.

freeze leftovers for quick soup

I keep a heavy-duty resealable plastic bag in the freezer to store soup ingredients. When we have corn, beans or other vegetables left over from dinner, I put them in the bag. I do the same with extra beef or chicken—even broth. In no time, I have everything I need to simmer up a nice soup. Since the vegetables are already cooked, I just add rice or noodles, and it's ready!

LEE D., LANSING, MICHIGAN

creamy asparagus chowder

SHIRLEY BEACHUM
SHELBY, MICHIGAN

While this soup is good with fresh asparagus, it can also be prepared with the frozen or canned variety. I like to blanch and freeze asparagus in portions just right for the recipe.

- 2 medium onions, chopped
- 2 cups chopped celery
- 1/4 cup butter
- 1 garlic clove, minced
- 1/2 cup all-purpose flour
- 1 large potato, peeled and cut into 1/2-inch cubes
- 4 cups milk
- 4 cups chicken broth
- 1/2 teaspoon dried thyme
- 1/2 teaspoon dried marjoram
- 4 cups chopped fresh asparagus, cooked and drained

Salt and pepper to taste
Sliced almonds
Shredded cheddar cheese
Chopped fresh tomato

1 In a Dutch oven, saute onions and celery in butter until tender. Add garlic; cook 1 minute longer. Stir in flour. Add the potato, milk, broth and herbs; cook over low heat, stirring occasionally, until the potato is tender and soup is thickened, about 20-30 minutes.

2 Add asparagus, salt and pepper; heat through. To serve, sprinkle with almonds, cheese and the chopped tomato.

YIELD: ABOUT 2-1/2 QUARTS.

sweet potato and pear soup

CRISTY SHANK
SUMMERSVILLE, WEST VIRGINIA

I'm a family physician who loves to try new recipes. This tasty cold-weather soup has garnered many warm compliments from family and friends. They simply rave over it!

- 1-3/4 pounds sweet potatoes (about 4 medium), peeled and cubed
- 1-3/4 cups water
- 1 teaspoon salt, *divided*
- 1/4 teaspoon ground cinnamon
- 2 large pears, peeled and sliced
- 1 large onion, chopped
- 2 tablespoons butter
- 1/2 cup white grape juice
- 1 cup half-and-half cream
- 1/4 teaspoon white pepper

1 In a large saucepan, combine the sweet potatoes, water, 3/4 teaspoon salt and cinnamon. Bring to a boil. Reduce heat; simmer, uncovered, for 15-20 minutes or until tender.

2 Meanwhile, in another large saucepan, cook and stir the pears and onion in butter over medium heat for 5 minutes. Stir in grape juice; bring to a boil. Reduce heat; simmer, uncovered, for 5 minutes. Stir into the sweet potato mixture. Cool slightly.

3 In a blender, cover and puree soup in batches; return all to the pan. Stir in the cream, pepper and remaining salt; heat through (do not boil).

YIELD: 5 SERVINGS.

cheesy corn chowder

LOLA COMER
MARYSVILLE, WASHINGTON

I've had this chowder recipe for many years, and the whole gang really enjoys its cheesy corn taste. It makes a big pot—enough for seconds!

- 6 bacon strips, chopped
- 3/4 cup chopped sweet onion
- 2-1/2 cups water
- 2-1/2 cups cubed peeled potatoes
- 2 cups sliced fresh carrots
- 2 teaspoons chicken bouillon granules
- 3 cans (11 ounces *each*) gold and white corn, drained
- 1/2 teaspoon pepper
- 7 tablespoons all-purpose flour
- 5 cups 2% milk
- 3 cups (12 ounces) shredded cheddar cheese
- 1 cup cubed process cheese (Velveeta)

1 In a Dutch oven, cook the bacon and onion over medium heat until the onion is tender. Add the water, potatoes, carrots and bouillon; bring to a boil. Reduce heat; cover and simmer for 15-20 minutes or until potatoes are tender.

2 Stir in corn and pepper. In a large bowl, whisk the flour and milk until smooth; add to the soup. Bring to a boil; cook and stir for 2 minutes or until thickened. Reduce the heat. Add the cheeses; cook and stir until cheeses are melted.

YIELD: 15 SERVINGS (3-3/4 QUARTS).

chunky potato soup

STEPHANIE MOON
BOISE, IDAHO

This creamy, satisfying soup instantly became our favorite. It's perfect on chilly days. Even those who don't normally like Swiss cheese savor each delicious sip.

- 4 medium potatoes (about 2 pounds), peeled and cubed
- 3/4 cup chopped onion
- 1 small carrot, chopped
- 1/4 cup chopped celery
- 1-1/2 cups chicken broth
- 3 tablespoons butter, cubed
- 3 tablespoons all-purpose flour
- 2-1/2 cups milk
- 1 tablespoon minced fresh parsley
- 3/4 teaspoon salt
- 1/2 teaspoon pepper
- 1 cup (4 ounces) shredded Swiss cheese

1 In a large saucepan, combine the potatoes, onion, carrot, celery and broth. Bring to a boil. Reduce the heat; cover and simmer for 12-15 minutes or until vegetables are tender; lightly mash.

2 Meanwhile, in a small saucepan, melt butter; stir in flour until smooth. Gradually stir in milk. Bring to a boil; cook and stir for 2 minutes or until thickened. Stir into the potato mixture. Cook and stir until thickened and bubbly. Add parsley, salt and pepper. Remove from the heat; stir in cheese until melted.

YIELD: 7 SERVINGS.

keep veggies on hand

When I buy fresh carrots, celery and onions, I chop them up, use what I need and then freeze the rest in small amounts. That way, I always have vegetables on hand for when I want to make soups, stews and casseroles.

JOAN F., COLUMBUS, OHIO

golden state mushroom soup

DAVID PATTON
SAN JOSE, CALIFORNIA

Mushrooms have become very popular in my area, but they've long been a favorite of mine. After years of searching for a good mushroom soup recipe, I gave up and created one of my own.

- 1 pound fresh mushrooms, sliced
- 1 medium onion, chopped
- 1/4 cup butter, cubed
- 1/4 cup all-purpose flour
- 1/2 teaspoon salt
- 1/8 teaspoon pepper
- 1-1/2 cups milk
- 1 can (14-1/2 ounces) chicken broth
- 1 teaspoon chicken bouillon granules
- 1 cup (8 ounces) sour cream

Minced fresh parsley, optional

1 In a large saucepan, saute mushrooms and onion in butter until tender. Stir in the flour, salt and pepper. Gradually stir in the milk, broth and bouillon; bring to a boil. Cook and stir for 2 minutes or until thickened. Reduce heat. Stir in sour cream; heat through (do not boil). Sprinkle with parsley if desired.

YIELD: 4-6 SERVINGS.

curried leek soup

ARNOLD FOSS
MERCER, MAINE

New England is known for its hearty soups. I like to experiment with recipes. (Luckily, I have a wife who lets me mess up her kitchen.) I came up with this recipe the first year I grew leeks in my garden.

- 3 medium leeks (white portion only), thinly sliced
- 2 tablespoons butter
- 1 garlic clove, minced
- 1 can (14-1/2 ounces) chicken broth
- 3/4 cup water
- 1-1/2 cups thinly sliced carrots
- 2 celery ribs, thinly sliced
- 2 teaspoons chicken bouillon granules
- 1/2 teaspoon curry powder
- 1/8 teaspoon pepper
- 1 can (12 ounces) fat-free evaporated milk

1 In a large saucepan, saute leeks in butter over medium heat until tender. Add garlic; cook 1 minute longer. Stir in the broth, water, carrots, celery, bouillon, curry powder and pepper. Bring to a boil.

2 Reduce heat; cover and simmer for 20-25 minutes or until vegetables are tender. Cool slightly.

3 Place 1 cup soup in a blender; cover and process until smooth. Return to the pan. Add the milk; heat through (do not boil).

YIELD: 4 SERVINGS.

chicken chowder

HEATHER HAMILTON
BUNKER HILL, WEST VIRGINIA

This is wonderful served over tortilla chips or with corn bread as a side. Packed with chicken and veggies, this chunky chowder makes a nutritious meal.

- 1 can (14-1/2 ounces) reduced-sodium chicken broth
- 1 can (10-3/4 ounces) condensed cream of chicken soup, undiluted
- 1 can (10-3/4 ounces) condensed cream of potato soup, undiluted
- 1-1/2 cups milk
- 2 cans (14-1/2 ounces *each*) diced tomatoes, undrained
- 2 cups cubed cooked chicken
- 1 can (11 ounces) Mexicorn, drained
- 1/3 cup chopped onion
- 1 can (4 ounces) chopped green chilies
- 1-1/2 cups (6 ounces) shredded Monterey Jack cheese

1 In a large saucepan, combine the broth, soups and milk. Stir in the tomatoes, chicken, Mexicorn, onion and chilies. Bring to a boil. Reduce heat; simmer, uncovered, for 10-15 minutes or until onion is tender. Garnish with cheese.

YIELD: 8 SERVINGS (3 QUARTS).

low-cholesterol soup

We need to watch our cholesterol, so I make a large batch of low-cholesterol soup. I start with dried beans, peas, barley and rice and add several seasonal vegetables and seasonings. I can keep the soup in a sealed container in the refrigerator for 3-4 days. To serve, I add some cubed cooked chicken breast, prepared earlier in the week to save time, to a portion of the soup and heat it up. This is a quick and easy way to use up leftovers and get lunch or dinner on the table during busy weekdays. And it helps us eat healthy when we are at our busiest!

ANN D., MINNEAPOLIS, MINNESOTA

corn and squash soup

JANICE ZOOK
WHITE RIVER JUNCTION, VERMONT

This rich soup pairs squash and cream-style corn. My family says this is their favorite squash recipe, and friends also comment on its wonderful flavor.

- 12 bacon strips, diced
- 1 medium onion, chopped
- 1 celery rib, chopped
- 2 tablespoons all-purpose flour
- 1 can (14-1/2 ounces) chicken broth
- 6 cups mashed cooked butternut squash
- 2 cans (8-3/4 ounces *each*) cream-style corn
- 2 cups half-and-half cream
- 1 tablespoon minced fresh parsley
- 1-1/2 teaspoons salt
- 1/2 teaspoon pepper
- Sour cream, optional

1 In a large saucepan, cook bacon over medium heat until crisp. Remove to paper towels; drain, reserving 2 tablespoons drippings.

2 In the drippings, saute onion and celery until tender. Stir in flour until blended. Gradually stir in broth. Bring to a boil; cook and stir for 2 minutes or until slightly thickened.

3 Reduce heat to medium. Stir in the squash, corn, cream, parsley, salt, pepper and bacon. Cook and stir until heated through. Garnish with sour cream if desired.

YIELD: 8 SERVINGS (2-1/2 QUARTS).

roasted red pepper bisque

MARY ANN ZETTLEMAIER
CHELSEA, MICHIGAN

Folks are sure to comment about the awesome roasted red pepper flavor of this velvety soup. It's a fantastic first course for special occasions or alongside sandwiches at a casual gathering.

- 8 medium sweet red peppers
- 1 large onion, chopped
- 2 tablespoons butter
- 3 cups chicken broth, *divided*
- 2 cups half-and-half cream
- 1/2 teaspoon salt
- 1/2 teaspoon white pepper
- 6 tablespoons shredded Parmesan cheese, *divided*

1 Broil peppers 4 in. from the heat until skins blister, about 5 minutes. With tongs, rotate peppers a quarter turn. Broil and rotate until all sides are blistered and blackened. Immediately place peppers in a large bowl; cover and let stand for 15-20 minutes.

2 Peel off and discard charred skin. Remove stems and seeds; set peppers aside.

3 In a large saucepan, saute onion in butter until tender; cool slightly. In a blender, combine onion mixture, 2 cups broth and roasted peppers; cover and process until smooth. Return to the pan.

4 Stir in cream and remaining broth; heat through (do not boil). Stir in salt and pepper. Sprinkle each serving with 1 tablespoon Parmesan cheese.

YIELD: 6 SERVINGS (2 QUARTS).

cheeseburger paradise soup

NADINA LADIMARCO
BURTON, OHIO

I've never met a person who didn't enjoy this creamy soup, and it's substantial enough to serve as a main course with your favorite bread or dinner rolls.

- 6 medium potatoes, peeled and cubed
- 1 small carrot, grated
- 1 small onion, chopped
- 1/2 cup chopped green pepper
- 2 tablespoons chopped seeded jalapeno pepper
- 3 cups water
- 2 tablespoons plus 2 teaspoons beef bouillon granules
- 2 garlic cloves, minced
- 1/8 teaspoon pepper
- 2 pounds ground beef
- 1/2 pound sliced fresh mushrooms
- 2 tablespoons butter
- 5 cups milk, *divided*
- 6 tablespoons all-purpose flour
- 1 package (16 ounces) process cheese (Velveeta), cubed

Crumbled cooked bacon

1 In a Dutch oven, combine the first nine ingredients; bring to a boil. Reduce heat; cover and simmer for 10-15 minutes or until potatoes are tender.

2 Meanwhile, in a large skillet, cook beef and mushrooms in butter over medium heat until meat is no longer pink; drain. Add to soup. Stir in 4 cups milk; heat through.

3 In a small bowl, combine flour and remaining milk until smooth; gradually stir into soup. Bring to a boil; cook and stir for 2 minutes or until thickened. Reduce heat; stir in cheese until melted. Garnish with bacon.

YIELD: 14 SERVINGS (ABOUT 3-1/2 QUARTS).

EDITOR'S NOTE: We recommend wearing disposable gloves when cutting hot peppers. Avoid touching your face.

sweet surprise chili

BROOKE PEKKALA
DULUTH, MINNESOTA

I've won three chili cook-offs with my recipe. Everyone loves it, and they're always amazed when I reveal the secret ingredient!

- 3 pounds beef top sirloin steak, cubed
- 1 tablespoon canola oil
- 1/2 pound bulk Italian sausage
- 1 large onion, chopped
- 5 garlic cloves, minced
- 2 cups water
- 1 can (16 ounces) chili beans, undrained
- 1 can (15 ounces) tomato sauce
- 1 can (14-1/2 ounces) beef broth
- 1 package (12 ounces) pitted dried plums, chopped
- 3 teaspoons chili powder
- 2 teaspoons ground cumin
- 1 teaspoon dried oregano
- 1 teaspoon paprika
- 3/4 teaspoon salt
- Dash cayenne pepper

1 In a Dutch oven, brown beef in oil in batches. Remove and keep warm.

Add sausage and onion to the pan; cook and stir over medium heat until meat is no longer pink. Add garlic; cook 1 minute longer.

2 Return beef to the pan; stir in the remaining ingredients. Bring to a boil. Reduce heat; cover and simmer for 1-3/4 to 2 hours or until beef is tender.

YIELD: 8 SERVINGS (2-3/4 QUARTS).

hot dog bean soup

MARY ANN KIME
STURGIS, MICHIGAN

My husband fixed this soup for our three kids years ago. They always loved it, and they now prepare it for their own kids. It's a real favorite on family camping trips.

- 3 hot dogs, halved lengthwise and cut into 1/4-inch pieces
- 1 teaspoon canola oil
- 1 can (16 ounces) kidney beans, rinsed and drained
- 1 can (11-1/2 ounces) condensed bean and bacon soup, undiluted
- 1-1/4 cups water
- 1 teaspoon dried minced onion
- 1/4 teaspoon pepper

1 In a large skillet, cook the hot dogs in oil over medium heat for 3-4 minutes or until browned.

2 Meanwhile, in a 2-qt. microwave-safe bowl, combine the remaining ingredients. Cover and microwave on high for 2-3 minutes or until heated through, stirring once. Stir in the hot dogs.

YIELD: 4 SERVINGS.

EDITOR'S NOTE: This recipe was tested in a 1,100-watt microwave.

jumpin' espresso bean chili

JESSIE APFEL
BERKELEY, CALIFORNIA

I got this idea after sampling different chili at various restaurants. Family and friends who have tried my creation said this recipe is definitely a keeper.

- 3 medium onions, chopped
- 2 tablespoons olive oil
- 2 tablespoons brown sugar
- 2 tablespoons chili powder
- 2 tablespoons ground cumin
- 1 tablespoon instant coffee granules
- 1 tablespoon baking cocoa
- 3/4 teaspoon salt
- 2 cans (14-1/2 ounces *each*) no-salt-added diced tomatoes
- 1 can (15 ounces) black beans, rinsed and drained
- 1 can (15 ounces) kidney beans, rinsed and drained
- 1 can (15 ounces) garbanzo beans *or* chickpeas, rinsed and drained

Sour cream, thinly sliced green onions, shredded cheddar cheese and pickled jalapeno slices, optional

1 In a Dutch oven, saute the onions in oil until tender. Add the brown sugar, chili powder, cumin, coffee granules, cocoa and salt; cook and stir for about 1 minute.

2 Stir in tomatoes and beans. Bring to a boil. Reduce heat; cover and simmer for 30 minutes or until heated through. Serve with sour cream, onions, cheese and jalapeno slices if desired.

YIELD: 7 SERVINGS.

chili 'n' cheese burritos

For a chili makeover, lightly coat a baking dish with cooking spray. Spoon the leftover chili into tortillas, roll up and place seam side down in the dish. Cover with shredded cheese and bake until the cheese melts and the chili is heated through. Serve with sour cream, chopped onions and black olives.

JILL S., ALEXANDRIA, INDIANA

speedy jambalaya

NICOLE FILIZETTI
GRAND MARAIS, MICHIGAN

Spicy sausage and colorful sweet peppers make this classic Cajun dish look as appetizing as it tastes. It's impossible to say no to seconds!

1-1/3 cups uncooked long grain rice
1 large onion, halved and sliced
1 medium green pepper, sliced
1 medium sweet red pepper, sliced
2 teaspoons olive oil
3 garlic cloves, minced
1 can (28 ounces) diced tomatoes, undrained

3 bay leaves
1 teaspoon salt
1 teaspoon paprika
1/2 teaspoon dried thyme
1/2 teaspoon pepper
1/4 teaspoon hot pepper sauce
2 cans (15-1/2 ounces *each*) black-eyed peas, rinsed and drained
3/4 pound fully cooked andouille *or* Italian sausage links, sliced
1/4 cup minced fresh parsley

1 Cook rice according to package directions. Meanwhile, in a large skillet, saute onion and peppers in oil for 4 minutes. Add garlic; cook 1 minute longer. Stir in the tomatoes, bay leaves, salt, paprika, thyme, pepper and pepper sauce. Bring to a boil.

2 Reduce heat; simmer, uncovered, for 5 minutes. Stir in peas and sausage; heat through. Discard bay leaves. Serve with rice. Sprinkle each serving with parsley.

YIELD: 8 SERVINGS.

sausage savvy

Andouille, a smoked sausage made of pork and garlic, is usually associated with favorite Cajun recipes like jambalaya and gumbo.

TASTE OF HOME TEST KITCHEN

three-bean taco chili

WANDA LEE
HEMET, CALIFORNIA

This hearty chili is filling, nourishing and tastes like it simmered all day long. Leftover chili freezes well for a later time, so why not make a double recipe to feed guests?

- 2 pounds ground beef
- 2 cups water
- 1 can (16 ounces) refried beans
- 1 can (16 ounces) kidney beans, rinsed and drained
- 1 can (16 ounces) chili beans, undrained
- 1 can (15-1/4 ounces) whole kernel corn, drained
- 1 can (14-1/2 ounces) stewed tomatoes
- 1 can (8 ounces) tomato sauce
- 1 cup chunky salsa
- 1 envelope taco seasoning
- 1 can (2-1/4 ounces) sliced ripe olives, drained
- 1 cup (4 ounces) shredded cheddar cheese

1 In a Dutch oven, cook beef over medium heat until no longer pink; drain. Stir in the water, beans, corn, tomatoes, tomato sauce, salsa, taco seasoning and olives.

2 Bring to a boil. Reduce heat; simmer, uncovered, for 10 minutes. Garnish with cheese.

YIELD: 9 SERVINGS.

meatball stew

JOAN CHASSE
BERLIN, CONNECTICUT

Rich and satisfying, this savory stew is chock-full of tender meatballs and veggies that are sure to warm you up when there's an autumn chill in the air.

- 3 eggs, lightly beaten
- 2/3 cup seasoned bread crumbs
- 1/3 cup grated Parmesan cheese
- Dash pepper
- 1/2 pound *each* ground beef, pork and veal
- 4 medium potatoes, peeled and cut into small chunks
- 3 medium carrots, sliced
- 1-1/2 cups chopped celery
- 1 medium onion, cut into wedges
- 1 garlic clove, minced
- 1 envelope onion soup mix
- 2-1/4 cups water
- 1 cup frozen peas, thawed
- 4-1/2 teaspoons minced fresh parsley

1 In a large bowl, combine the eggs, bread crumbs, cheese and pepper. Crumble beef, pork and veal over mixture and mix well. Shape into 1-1/2-in. balls.

2 Place meatballs on a greased rack in a shallow baking pan. Bake at 350° for 20-25 minutes or until no longer pink. Drain on paper towels.

3 Place the meatballs, potatoes, carrots, celery, onion and garlic in a Dutch oven. In a small bowl, combine soup mix and water; pour over meatball mixture. Bring to a boil. Reduce heat; cover and simmer for 25-30 minutes or until vegetables are tender. Stir in peas and parsley; heat through.

YIELD: 10 SERVINGS (2-1/2 QUARTS).

chunky beef stew

TASTE OF HOME TEST KITCHEN

You don't need to simmer homemade stew for hours when you use a more tender cut of beef, like sirloin steak. This stick-to-your-ribs dish is wonderful after a day of sledding or skating.

- 1 pound beef sirloin steak, cut into 1/2-inch cubes
- 3 medium carrots, sliced
- 4 celery ribs, sliced
- 1 small onion, chopped
- 2 tablespoons canola oil
- 2 cans (14-1/2 ounces *each*) beef broth
- 2 garlic cloves, minced
- 1 teaspoon dried rosemary, crushed
- 3/4 teaspoon pepper
- 1/4 cup cornstarch
- 1/4 cup cold water
- 1 teaspoon browning sauce, optional

1 In a Dutch oven, cook the beef, carrots, celery and onion in oil until beef is browned; drain. Add the broth, garlic, rosemary and pepper. Bring to a boil. Reduce heat; cover and simmer for 12-15 minutes or until beef and vegetables are tender.

2 Combine the cornstarch and water until smooth; gradually stir into beef mixture. Bring to a boil; cook and stir for 2 minutes or until thickened. Add browning sauce if desired.

YIELD: 6 SERVINGS.

terrific turkey chili

KIM SEEGER
BROOKLYN PARK, MINNESOTA

Here's a satisfying medley that's full of zesty tomatoes and provides a good bit of fiber. Top it with reduced-fat cheese, cilantro and green onions.

- 1 pound lean ground turkey
- 1 cup chopped onion
- 1 cup chopped green pepper
- 2 teaspoons minced garlic
- 1 can (28 ounces) crushed tomatoes
- 1 can (16 ounces) kidney beans, rinsed and drained
- 1 can (11-1/2 ounces) tomato juice
- 1 can (6 ounces) tomato paste
- 1 can (4 ounces) chopped green chilies
- 2 tablespoons brown sugar
- 1 tablespoon dried parsley flakes
- 1 tablespoon ground cumin
- 3 teaspoons chili powder
- 2 teaspoons dried oregano
- 1-1/2 teaspoons pepper

1 In a large saucepan, cook the turkey, onion, green pepper and garlic over medium heat until meat is no longer pink; drain.

2 Stir in the remaining ingredients. Bring to a boil. Reduce heat; cover and simmer for 25 minutes.

YIELD: 6 SERVINGS (ABOUT 2 QUARTS).

stew or goulash?

Any dish prepared by stewing—simmering food in liquid for a long time in a covered pot—can be considered stew. Stew most often refers to a main dish that contains meat, vegetables and a thick broth made from the stewing juices. Goulash is a kind of stew, usually of Hungarian origin, made with meat and vegetables and seasoned with paprika.

TASTE OF HOME TEST KITCHEN

pueblo green chili stew

HELEN LABRAKE
RINDGE, NEW HAMPSHIRE

Green chilies add a little spice to my flavorful pork stew, which also features corn, potatoes and tomatoes.

- 2 pounds lean boneless pork, cut into 1-1/2 inch cubes
- 1 tablespoon canola oil
- 3 cans (11 ounces *each*) whole kernel corn, drained
- 2 celery ribs, chopped
- 2 medium potatoes, peeled and chopped
- 2 medium tomatoes, coarsely chopped
- 3 cans (4 ounces *each*) chopped green chilies
- 4 cups chicken broth
- 2 teaspoons ground cumin
- 1 teaspoon dried oregano
- 1 teaspoon salt, optional

1 In a large Dutch oven, brown the pork in batches in oil over medium-high heat. Add the remaining ingredients. Bring to a boil. Reduce the heat; cover and simmer for 1 hour or until pork is tender.

YIELD: 8 SERVINGS (ABOUT 2-1/2 QUARTS).

reading meat labels

Meat labels provide you a variety of information. They tell you the type of meat (beef, pork, veal or lamb), the wholesale cut (loin, rib, shoulder, leg, etc.) and the retail cut (steak, chops, roast, etc.). The label also has the sell-by date, the weight of the meat, cost per pound and total price. Tenderness helps determine an appropriate cooking method. Tender cuts are best cooked with dry heat (grilling, broiling, roasting, pan-frying, pan-broiling or stir-frying). Less tender cuts are better cooked by moist heat (braising or cooking in liquid).

TASTE OF HOME TEST KITCHEN

chicken stew

TASTE OF HOME TEST KITCHEN

Want a luscious stew with tender chicken and veggies in a creamy gravy? There are only a handful of ingredients in my recipe, but it still delivers that old-fashioned flavor. Serve it with grilled cheese, or with fresh-from-the-oven biscuits.

- 1 pound boneless skinless chicken breasts, cut into 1-inch cubes
- 1 tablespoon olive oil
- 1 package (16 ounces) frozen vegetables for stew
- 1 jar (12 ounces) chicken gravy
- 1/2 teaspoon dried thyme
- 1/4 teaspoon rubbed sage
- 1/4 teaspoon pepper

1 In a large saucepan, brown chicken in oil over medium heat for 4-6 minutes or until no longer pink. Drain if necessary.

2 Stir in the remaining ingredients. Bring to a boil. Reduce heat; cover and simmer for 15 minutes or until vegetables are tender.

YIELD: 4 SERVINGS.

california pepper chili

ROBYN THOMPSON
LOS ANGELES, CALIFORNIA

In my opinion, this is the world's best chili! It features three meats in a peppery, eye-opening broth.

- 1/2 pound bacon, diced
- 2-1/2 pounds beef stew meat, cut into 3/4-inch cubes
- 1-1/2 pounds pork stew meat, cut into 3/4-inch cubes
- 2 medium onions, chopped
- 6 to 8 garlic cloves, minced
- 1 to 2 tablespoons chopped seeded fresh serrano chili peppers
- 1 to 2 tablespoons chopped seeded fresh poblano chili peppers
- 1 to 2 tablespoons chopped seeded fresh jalapeno peppers
- 2 to 3 teaspoons cayenne pepper
- 1-1/2 teaspoons dried oregano
- 1 teaspoon salt
- 1 teaspoon ground cumin
- 1 can (15 ounces) tomato puree
- 1 can (14-1/2 ounces) beef broth
- 7 plum tomatoes, chopped

Shredded cheddar cheese, optional

1 In a Dutch oven, cook bacon over medium heat until crisp. Using a slotted spoon, remove to paper towels; drain, reserving 3 tablespoons drippings.

2 In the drippings, cook the beef, pork and onions until meat is no longer pink; drain. Add the garlic, peppers and seasonings; cook and stir for 1-2 minutes.

3 Stir in the tomato puree, broth and tomatoes. Bring to a boil. Reduce heat; cover and simmer for 1 to 1-1/2 hours or until meat is tender. Garnish with reserved bacon and cheese if desired.

YIELD: 10 SERVINGS (2-1/2 QUARTS).

EDITOR'S NOTE: We recommend wearing disposable gloves when cutting hot peppers. Avoid touching your face.

individual campfire stew

MARGARET RILEY
TALLAHASSEE, FLORIDA

These little packs are great for grilling or whipping up over a campfire. I can get several outdoor chores done while they're cooking.

- 1 egg, lightly beaten
- 3/4 cup dry bread crumbs
- 1/4 cup ketchup
- 1 tablespoon Worcestershire sauce
- 1 teaspoon seasoned salt
- 1 pound lean ground beef (90% lean)
- 2 cups frozen shredded hash brown potatoes, thawed
- 1 cup diced carrots
- 1 cup condensed cream of chicken soup, undiluted
- 1/4 cup milk

1 Prepare grill for indirect heat. In a large bowl, combine the first five ingredients. Crumble beef over mixture and mix well. Shape into four patties. Place each patty on a greased double thickness of heavy-duty foil (about 12 in. square); sprinkle each with potatoes and carrots.

2 Combine soup and milk; spoon over meat and vegetables. Fold foil around mixture and seal tightly. Grill, covered, over indirect medium heat for 25-30 minutes or until a meat thermometer reads 160° and juices run clear. Open foil carefully to allow steam to escape.

YIELD: 4 SERVINGS.

pepperoni pizza chili

MARILOUISE WYATT
COWEN, WEST VIRGINIA

I came up with this recipe one day when I was craving pizza but didn't want to fuss with making a crust. I just put the pizza in a bowl instead!

- 1 pound ground beef
- 1 can (16 ounces) kidney beans, rinsed and drained
- 1 can (15 ounces) pizza sauce
- 1 can (14-1/2 ounces) Italian stewed tomatoes
- 1 can (8 ounces) tomato sauce
- 1-1/2 cups water
- 1 package (3-1/2 ounces) sliced pepperoni
- 1/2 cup chopped green pepper
- 1 teaspoon pizza seasoning *or* Italian seasoning
- 1 teaspoon salt

Shredded part-skim mozzarella cheese, optional

1 In a large saucepan, cook beef over medium heat until no longer pink; drain. Stir in the beans, pizza sauce, tomatoes, tomato sauce, water, pepperoni, green pepper, pizza seasoning and salt. Bring to a boil.

2 Reduce heat; simmer, uncovered, for 30 minutes or until chili reaches desired thickness. Sprinkle with cheese if desired.

YIELD: 8 SERVINGS (2 QUARTS).

turkey noodle stew

TRACI MALONEY
TOMS RIVER, NEW JERSEY

I can assemble my stew, a creamy mixture of turkey, vegetables and noodles, in minutes. My husband doesn't usually go for meal-in-one dishes, but he likes this savory skillet entree.

- 2 turkey breast tenderloins (about 1/2 pound *each*), cut into 1/4-inch slices
- 1 medium onion, chopped
- 1 tablespoon canola oil
- 1 can (14-1/2 ounces) chicken broth
- 1 can (10-3/4 ounces) condensed cream of celery soup, undiluted
- 2 cups frozen mixed vegetables
- 1/2 to 1 teaspoon lemon-pepper seasoning
- 3 cups uncooked extra-wide egg noodles

1 In a large skillet, cook turkey and onion in oil for 5-6 minutes or until turkey is no longer pink; drain.

2 In a large bowl, combine the broth, soup, vegetables and lemon-pepper. Add to the skillet; bring to a boil. Stir in noodles. Reduce heat; cover and simmer for 10 minutes or until noodles and vegetables are tender.

YIELD: 6 SERVINGS.

mediterranean chicken stew

TASTE OF HOME TEST KITCHEN

Tomatoes and peppers lend some eye-catching color to a quick-to-fix stew. The mild seasonings will appeal to everyone's tastes.

- 1 medium onion, chopped
- 2 garlic cloves, minced
- 2 tablespoons canola oil
- 1-1/2 pounds boneless skinless chicken breasts, cut into 1-inch pieces
- 2 cans (14-1/2 ounces *each*) stewed tomatoes
- 1 medium green pepper, julienned
- 1 medium sweet red pepper, julienned
- 1 cup pitted ripe olives
- 1 teaspoon salt
- 1 teaspoon dried oregano
- 2 tablespoons cornstarch
- 3 tablespoons cold water

Hot cooked rice

1 In a large skillet, saute onion and garlic in oil for 3-4 minutes or until tender. Add chicken; cook for 6-8 minutes or until no longer pink. Stir in the tomatoes, peppers, olives, salt and oregano; bring to a boil. Reduce heat; cover and simmer for 10-12 minutes, stirring occasionally.

2 Combine cornstarch and water until smooth; gradually stir into chicken mixture. Bring to a boil; cook and stir for 1 minute or until thickened. Serve with rice.

YIELD: 6 SERVINGS.

creamy white chili

LAURA BREWER
LAFAYETTE, INDIANA

My sister-in-law made a big batch of chili to serve a crowd one night. It was a hit. The recipe is easy and quick, which is helpful since I'm a college student. In all my years of cooking, I've never had another dish get so many compliments.

- 1 pound boneless skinless chicken breasts, cut into 1/2-inch cubes
- 1 medium onion, chopped
- 1-1/2 teaspoons garlic powder
- 1 tablespoon canola oil
- 2 cans (15-1/2 ounces *each*) great northern beans, rinsed and drained
- 1 can (14-1/2 ounces) chicken broth
- 2 cans (4 ounces *each*) chopped green chilies
- 1 teaspoon salt
- 1 teaspoon ground cumin
- 1 teaspoon dried oregano
- 1/2 teaspoon pepper
- 1/4 teaspoon cayenne pepper
- 1 cup (8 ounces) sour cream
- 1/2 cup heavy whipping cream

1 In a large saucepan, saute the chicken, onion and garlic powder in oil until chicken is no longer pink. Add the beans, broth, chilies and seasonings. Bring to a boil. Reduce heat; simmer, uncovered, for 30 minutes.

2 Remove from the heat; stir in sour cream and cream.

YIELD: 7 SERVINGS.

EDITOR'S NOTE: You may substitute half-and-half cream for the heavy cream if desired.

GENERAL RECIPE INDEX

This index lists every recipe by major ingredient so you can easily locate recipes to suit your needs.
An alphabetical index begins on page 111.

ALPHABETICAL INDEX